Workplace Intervention

"Dr. Fearing rallies us to save our most important assets: people."

—FERRIS THOMPSON
Vice President Corporate Partnerships, Universal Studios

"*Workplace Intervention* offers bottom-line advice. Every manager should read it."

—DAVE ANDERSON
Founder and Chairman of the Board,
Famous Dave's of America Restaurants

Workplace Intervention

The Bottom Line
on Helping Addicted Employees
Become Productive Again

James Fearing, Ph.D.

with a foreword by William D. Dunlap

HAZELDEN®

INFORMATION & EDUCATIONAL SERVICES

Hazelden
Center City, Minnesota 55012-0176

1-800-328-0094
1-651-213-4590 (Fax)
www.hazelden.org

Library of Congress Cataloging-in-Publication Data

Fearing, James, 1955–
    Workplace intervention : the bottom line on helping addicted
    employees become productive again / James Fearing ; with a
    foreword by William D. Dunlap.
        p. cm.
    Includes bibliographical references and index.
    ISBN 1-56838-520-X (paperback)
        1. Drugs and employment—United States. 2. Alcoholism and
    employment—United States. 3. Employee assistance programs—
    United States. I. Title.

HF5549.5.D7 F43 2000
658.3'822—dc21

                                                    00-044999

Author's note
The stories in this book are based on real people and actual business
situations. Details have been changed to preserve anonymity, and
some of the stories are composites of more than one person.

04 03 02 01 00   6 5 4 3 2 1

Cover design by Terri Kinne
Interior design by Donna Burch
Typesetting by Stanton Publication Services, Inc.

Contents

Foreword

The greatest menace to the American economy looms not on some distant continent, but within our own plants, stores, and offices. That menace is addiction, in all its forms and fury. The statistics tell the story. One in every ten employees has a drinking problem. A third of them do drugs. Nineteen million Americans suffer from depression, much of it drug and alcohol-related. And workplace violence, which follows the rising tide of employee substance abuse, is reaching epidemic proportions. One in every four acts of workplace violence involves drugs or alcohol. As business leaders, managers, and concerned citizens, we can't wait on the sidelines while the malignant forces of addiction drain the life out of our companies. It is time to act.

Dr. James Fearing shares this sense of urgency. After intervening on literally hundreds of addicts throughout the world, from CEOs to line employees, he has walked in the shadows where most of us dare not tread. If he has learned anything from those experiences, it is that waiting for employees to bottom out before offering them help is a terrible waste of human potential. Dr. Fearing is convinced that early intervention is one of corporate America's best defenses against the spread of addiction. After observing success with employees and colleagues, I wholeheartedly agree. In fact, when intervention is paired with clinical treatment and ongoing recovery programs, it is remarkably successful in arresting the disease. Chemical addiction may not be curable, but it is both treatable and preventable.

Alcoholics and addicts themselves cannot halt the spiral of addiction on their own. The denial factor makes that impossible. Nor can their families or friends, who often are unwitting victims. It is often up to employers, who carry the largest share of the financial burden, to take the lead. They are in a unique position to compel change. It is incumbent upon them to use this leverage for the good of the addicted employee, the rest of the workforce, their customers, and their shareholders. Everyone benefits when addicted employees become productive again.

Left untreated, addiction causes more deaths, illnesses, and disabilities than any other preventable health condition in corporate America. It is a stubborn disease that won't go away on its own. If anything, it worsens over time. Addiction feeds on benign neglect, claiming more hostages with each passing day. *Workplace Intervention* is a call to arms for all employees, business owners, and managers who want to reclaim lost employees. The book teaches them how to identify the patterns of abuse, address objectionable behavior, and know where and when to seek help. It does not attempt to make clinicians out of managers, but puts organizations back in charge of their employees' welfare, health, and safety. Workers expect this kind of involvement. The U.S. economy demands it.

American business has a serious substance abuse problem. Workplace intervention is the first step on the road to recovery. It saves companies money, improves overall productivity, bolsters morale, and ultimately saves lives. THAT IS THE BOTTOM LINE.

WILLIAM D. DUNLAP
Chairman, Campbell Mithun Esty

Acknowledgments

My work with companies and employees in crisis provided the original motivation to write a book on workplace intervention. The book is designed to help business owners, managers, and co-workers recognize and proactively address employee alcoholism, drug addiction, and other destroyers of human potential. It's also intended to guide human resources and employee assistance professionals who deal with these issues daily. The book offers knowledge, insight, and encouragement in the fight against addiction. The messages are applicable to every size businesses, from start-ups to Global 2000 operations. The time to take action is now. Early intervention saves lives and keeps organizations healthy and productive. That's the bottom line.

This book has been a pleasure to write. I would like to extend special thanks to several people who were instrumental in getting it published. My family—Colleen, Danny, and Kelly—was incredibly supportive throughout the process. I could not have done the work without my editor, the talented Anne Hunter. She was there every step of the way, and her understanding of the subject matter was key. Jeff Pauley, Ron Armstrong, and Louise Woehrle were superbly helpful from start to finish. To Barry Garfinkle, M.D., John Morgan, and Trent Tucker, thanks for your guidance and friendship. My editor at Hazelden, Richard Solly, provided great insight and professionalism. He set the standards of excellence. Last, I want to thank the many companies and their employees who I have had the pleasure of helping throughout the past decade. They gave me the inspiration and perspective to turn real-life crises into valuable learning tools.

1

The Cost of Addiction

Alcohol and drug abuse in today's workplace has reached epidemic proportions. More than one in ten employees have some kind of drinking problem. Almost a third of these drinkers also use illegal drugs. The prevalence of prescription drug abuse is on the rise too, with 30 percent of drug users turning to pharmacies to feed their habits. No matter which statistic you reference, the conclusion is the same: American business has a major substance abuse problem. It's pervasive, touching every industry at every level, and it won't go away on its own. The trouble is that most companies are ill prepared to deal with the problem. They don't know how to recognize the symptoms, let alone treat the illness. In some cases, they aren't even interested in trying.

Most people have no idea how costly untreated addiction can be to an organization or the economy. The total loss in productivity, profits, and overall performance is staggering—topping $102 billion in 1995.[1] The toll on human life is equally staggering. Users often forfeit their jobs, families, health, and lives to the insidious disease of addiction. Their co-workers, families, and friends suffer as well. Addiction is a social disease that casts a dark shadow over even the best of relationships. It robs people of their judgment and self-control. It steals their dignity. Addiction feeds off unrealized potential.

The invisible victims of workplace addiction are consumers. They buy consumables every day—from baby food to prescriptions—that carry the risk of contamination by impaired workers. They purchase cars, power tools, and appliances—any of which could inflict injury if improperly assembled by a worker under the influence. Consumers routinely put their lives in the hands of pilots, physicians, and other professionals, none of whom is beyond the long arm of addiction. Alcohol and drug abuse are equal opportunity diseases. They know no boundaries and respect no titles.

A phenomenon called the "disinhibitory factor" causes employees who are drunk, high, or stoned to lose their inhibitions and do things that are either inappropriate or downright dangerous. People and organizations get hurt in the process. Feeling free from normal constraints and responsibilities, these employees may sexually harass coworkers, share trade secrets with competitors, or neglect critical deadlines. Besides ignoring their duties as parents or driving recklessly, they may have affairs or inappropriate sexual relations at the workplace or engage in unsafe sex with strangers. The disinhibitory factor makes them feel invincible, so they take greater risks.

The more lines that chemical-abusing employees cross, the higher the cost to businesses and society. A forklift driver is more prone to accidents if he or she has a beer or two at lunch. A tool and die operator who smokes a joint with buddies after work will take greater risks and more shortcuts. Too often, their behavior results in a flawed product or a trip to the emergency room. Staff who overindulge at the company picnic and drive themselves home put themselves, other drivers, and their company at risk. The connection between drinking and driving is well established, but it's often overlooked in figuring the cost of addiction to American businesses.

Workplace addiction plays out in even less obvious ways. Alcohol and drugs contribute to one in every four acts of violence on the job. These outbreaks aren't as dramatic as the gun rampages dominating the headlines in recent years, but they are more frequent. They include arguments over the copy machine, fights in the lunchroom, physical destruction of property, theft, contamination or erasure of computer files, sabotage, threats, and other ways of acting out or getting even. All told, more than a million cases of workplace violence are reported in American businesses each year.

Although alcohol and drug addicts differ in their choice of chemicals, their disruptive effect in the workplace is the same—except where the law is concerned. Alcohol is a deadly, albeit legal drug. Despite shifts in public sentiment, it still carries an aura of social acceptability. Illicit drugs, on the other hand, are both deadly and illegal. They carry no such halo of indemnity. In fact, they are typically condemned as a social evil. People who use or possess drugs at work expose their employers to the risk of legal intervention—including raids, arrests, shutdowns, fines, and a bevy of legal entanglements. When any of these things happen, workplace morale and productivity plummet. Customers and vendors are scared off. The fallout creates a general sense of chaos and uncertainty in even the best-run organizations. Drug-related incidents at work also play on the growing public anxiety over crime and violence. The workplace, once considered a safe haven from extreme antisocial behavior, is no longer so.

Numbers Behind the Disease

- More than 11 million people in the workforce are considered "heavy drinkers," consuming at least five drinks a night, almost every day of the week.[2]

- Almost three-quarters of the nation's adult drug-using population was on a payroll in 1997.[3]

- Two out of three adults in the United States know someone who has gone to work under the influence of drugs and/or alcohol.[4]

- Substance-abusing employees are responsible for more than 40 percent of all industrial fatalities and nearly half of all industrial injuries.[5]

Terminology of Addiction

Counselors, clinicians, and professionals have their own vocabulary to describe the abuse or illegal use of alcohol, drugs, or other controlled substances. Each word reflects different nuances in meaning, many of which are lost on a lay audience. For simplicity, this book uses the terms *alcoholism, drug use* or *drug addiction, alcohol* or *chemical addiction, substance abuse,* and *chemical* or *alcohol dependency* interchangeably.

A Case for Business Intervention

In the face of this dark news, there is a bright light. Unlike AIDS, Alzheimer's, and other diseases without cures, substance abuse is treatable. It's also preventable. According to the Institute for Health Policy at Brandeis University, alcohol and drug addiction is "one of the top preventable health problems in the country."[6]

Imagine how long a company would last if it didn't prevent or halt business practices that contributed to ongoing financial losses. For compelling reasons, businesses need to get involved in the prevention or treatment of addiction:

- *Businesses have the most to lose when the disease goes untreated.* Review the sidebar "Putting a Price on Addiction" to help you assess the cost to your company of ignoring addiction in the workplace. Businesses of any size can no longer afford to lose talent to illnesses, especially during periods of full employment and worker shortages. Businesses benefit when an employee moves into recovery.
- *The price of ignoring addiction is too high.* Untreated alcoholism and addiction result in more deaths, illnesses, and disabilities than any other preventable health condition in corporate America. They can spread through an entire organization, destroying both its muscle and soul. Unchecked, they can strike a devastating blow to even the healthiest business.
- *People bring their addiction to work.* Addiction can't be compartmentalized. People don't cease being addicts when they leave home. They don't stop being sick when they punch the time clock each morning or sit down at their desk. Success lies in working in tandem with families and friends to arrest the illness.

The Cost of Employee Addiction

The hard costs of workplace addiction are staggering. And they're climbing at an alarming rate. Addiction costs go well beyond health care premiums and claims. They include hidden items like substance-related accidents, absenteeism, theft, medical liabilities, and low productivity.

For companies like General Motors, the tab approaches

$1 billion a year.[7] Every new car buyer contributes the equivalent of three full car payments to offset the cost of drug abuse in the plants and executive suites. For small businesses, the cost is tough to tally but just as weighty. Addiction-related costs of products, materials, and services get passed down the consumer chain, raising the price of doing business for everyone. A childcare center has to absorb inflated costs of insurance and compliance triggered by addiction elsewhere in the economy. A family-owned hardware store has to pay an invisible premium on inventory and shipping for the same reason. The cost of addiction worms its way into every pocket of the American economy, leaching the profits of businesses large and small. Everyone shoulders the burden.

Putting a Price on Addiction

- The total cost of alcohol and drug abuse in America has surpassed $250 billion.[8]
- A whopping $102 billion was attributable directly to corporate America.[9]
- Alcoholism causes more than 500 million lost workdays each year in the United States.[10]

When the price of addiction is understood, executives and line workers alike are shocked by the numbers. Until they start running the totals, most corporations have no idea how much money is being sucked down the drain of addiction. The dollar signs are too big to ignore.

Tallying the Human Deficit

Like many business executives with a social conscience and a bottom line imperative, Ruben, the human resources director of a Pennsylvania oil refinery, was concerned about the cost of addiction in his operation. He had a notion that the dollar figure was sizeable, so he asked his staff to examine the degree to which the refinery and its subsidiaries were affected by chemical and alcohol addiction. After months of gathering information and testing models, they presented their findings. The direct cost of substance abuse and dependence was conservatively estimated at more than $2 million a year.

Ruben was stunned. The cost to human lives and personal dignity, not to mention business profits, was enormous. Shortly thereafter, Ruben oversaw the start of a mandatory employee education program, the establishment of a professionally staffed employee assistance program, and the installation of a confidential crisis hot line for employees and their families. The results were significant, if not immediate. The company's estimated return on investment was ten to one.

The Addict among Us

Contrary to conventional wisdom, most untreated addicts and alcoholics are actively employed.[11] They hold jobs in offices, plants, hospitals, and stores. They work in service industries, manufacturing, the trades, and professions, crossing every educational and economic level. They count themselves among the ranks of hourly employees, middle managers, and top executives. Rarely do they fit the public stereotype of someone who lives under a bridge, sleeps in a park, and hasn't held a job for years.

Although most alcoholics and addicts are not literally on skid row, they spend many of their waking hours in a skid row state of mind. They bring their disease to work with them every day. Their co-workers and supervisors are affected most directly by their lack of performance, dysfunctional behavior, or poor work habits. The productivity and morale of people around them suffer. Vendors and customers also feel the backlash. Product quality and reliability deteriorate, putting consumers at risk and driving up costs.

Some companies combat the problem by establishing employee assistance programs (EAPs), either internally or through independent outside providers. In fact, almost a third of American workers have access to EAP services.[12] (Chapter 4 has more information about the role of EAPs.) Unfortunately, only 10 percent of the people who need EAP services ever access them. Many people avoid getting help through work-related services for four main reasons:

- *Fear of retribution.* Employees are reluctant to tap into official channels of support for fear of retribution or breach of confidentiality. That's why independently run hot lines are so effective. They are perceived to be more anonymous.

- *Denial.* Many people who struggle with addiction simply don't believe that they need help. Often, they think they can handle the problem on their own. Self-help can work in the short term but rarely leads to long-term recovery.

- *Lack of awareness.* Most employees don't know enough about addiction or recovery to make informed decisions. Nor are they familiar with what EAPs offer or how they work. Education is the answer here.

- *Fear of being labeled.* People are under the mistaken impression that everyone who goes through a chemical use assessment comes out "a confirmed addict." The reality is that a quarter to a half of the people who undergo assessments don't fit the criteria for addiction.

Assessing Organizational Tolerance for Drinking

Every organization has what I call a "drinking acceptability policy" (DAP). It may be formally written or tacitly understood. The DAP dictates how big a part, if any, alcohol plays in an organization's day-to-day work life. It's changed dramatically since the 1950s, when two-martini lunches were more the norm and addiction was less understood.

In assessing an organization's drinking acceptability policy, human resource managers need to begin interviewing line employees and middle management, not executives. Lower level employees have a clearer view of the problem, which tends to camouflage itself as it moves up the corporate ladder. This is especially true for large organizations, where the distance between the top and bottom rungs is great.

In a four-year study of Fortune 500 companies,[13] Harvard University researchers found that one-fourth of workday drinking in America goes on at the upper levels. The higher the level, the more acceptable workday drinking is. By comparison, only a sliver of daytime drinking happens among hourly employees. The reason is that upper managers have more freedom over their time and activities than their counterparts on the line and in the administrative pool. Managers' jobs don't require them to be accountable on an hour-to-hour basis. For them, lunchtime drinking may be both normal and acceptable. In fact, it accounts for the majority of all workday drinking in this country.

Even when it's done in moderation, lunchtime drinking has a negative effect on productivity. One glass of beer or wine with a hamburger may impair an employee's performance. People delude themselves by thinking that "a little won't hurt." It only takes a small amount of alcohol to blur clarity, retard reactions, and alter decision-making abilities.

The End of an Era

An East Coast advertising agency, concerned about its attitude toward drinking, decided to assess its current drinking acceptability policy. The agency's human resources staff began by investigating how their employees perceived the role of alcohol in the organization. Using an outside consultant, they met with dozens of people at all levels and employees from the top down believed that it was okay—even desirable—to mix liquor and business.

Over the next several months, HR worked to alter this perception. It wasn't easy. Alcohol played a big part in client courtship and retention. Bar tabs were standard on executives' expense accounts, and clients had been conditioned to expect expensive wine and liqueurs around the holidays.

With the encouragement of senior management and working with a volunteer policy team from every department, HR moved into action. They began by cleaning out every liquor cabinet in the place. This was no small task. Bars were standard equipment in conference rooms and most of the executive suites.

They drafted a clear policy on work-related drinking, which prohibited employees from drinking alcohol or using illicit drugs on company property or company time and driving company vehicles while under the influence.

Before the policy went into effect, the authors made a concerted effort to communicate it to employees at every level. A few objected, but most understood that public opinion no longer supported drinking alcohol in the workplace, and that the cost of mixing chemicals and work had become too great. The HR team made it clear that the policy applied to all employees, from the CEO to the mail clerk. Senior management agreed and publicly supported the change.

As part of the communication phase, employees were coached on how to break the news to clients, especially those who expected alcohol as a matter of course. Staff addressed the issue one-on-one, making a bottom-line case. They focused on how the change benefited clients— by improving agency productivity, creativity, and responsiveness, and by reducing hidden costs of addiction that ultimately are passed along in the form of higher fees and overhead. Most clients applauded their efforts. A few even asked for a copy of the policy so they could implement it in their own businesses.

Within a few months, the corporate culture began to shift. People replaced their alcohol-dependent habits with new, alcohol-free traditions. When a creative team landed a $1 million natural foods account, the staff celebrated by catering in a healthy lunch rather than clanking champagne glasses.

The agency is now a healthier, more focused place to work. The no-alcohol policy improved the agency's quality of work, level of client satisfaction, and staff retention. Costs are down and productivity is up.

Chronic Mismanagement

If identifying workplace substance abuse is challenging, managing it is nearly impossible. Hesitant to intrude on their employees' private lives, supervisors and managers naturally resist the need to confront the problem until action becomes unavoidable. They are apt to act only when an employee is openly intoxicated or disruptive, not before. The problem may have to escalate to a

crisis to warrant intervention. Respect for privacy, coupled with a legitimate concern over legal liability, feeds
their reluctance to take any action to resolve drug or alcohol issues at work.

Some avoid confronting an employee because they
don't know how to approach the problem. Sometimes
this stems from a lack of understanding of the disease.
Just as often, it results from a lack of training. Unless
people have been instructed on the intervention process,
they generally have no idea where to begin. Intervention
is not taught in high schools or colleges. Nor is it part of
most company training programs. What people do know
they learn in the school of hard knocks. It's not the most
reliable teacher.

Once addiction spills into the workplace, it is no longer
a private issue. It impacts other employees, customers, and
the community where the company does business. That's
why managers have an obligation to get involved. Even
those who accept that alcoholism and drug addiction are
diseases frequently stumble and hesitate here. Despite
book knowledge to the contrary, they still expect alcoholics
or addicts to possess the wherewithal to handle the illness
on their own—without the help of company or health care
professionals. They believe that reprimands, pep talks, or
expulsion can remedy addiction.

These responses, while common, are neither effective
nor appropriate. They reflect a misguided thinking that is
deep-seated in the American culture. Although the
American Medical Association defined alcohol and drug
abuse as a "disease" in the 1950s, many still consider addiction a moral failing or the result of a lack of willpower.
Even today, some branches of the U.S. military still deny
educational and medical benefits to veterans with addictions, citing evidence of "wrongful misconduct" as justi-
fication. Attitudes sometimes take generations to change.

Untreated alcoholism and addiction can shipwreck even the most promising careers. The closer the addict is to the captain's quarters, the slower he or she is to recognize the distress signals. When people around them fail to send out the lifeboats, disaster ensues.

A Shipwrecked Career

John was a broker in a highly successful capital management firm that managed more than $1 billion in assets every year. Unfortunately, John had a serious addiction to alcohol and cocaine. After years of habitual use, his behavior became erratic and out of control. He lost his ability to make good decisions and manage the financial affairs of his clients. Eventually, his colleagues and clients lost confidence in him. So did his boss. In 1998, after losing more than half of his clientele, he was asked to resign.

No one in John's life stepped forward to help him. Neither his peers nor the executive team intervened. His wife filed for divorce. His friends drifted away. The cost of his addiction, personally and professionally, was enormous. He lived with the pain and shame of being fired by colleagues who once had held him in high esteem. His physical health suffered. By the time he received help, he was near death, having suffered three seizures in as many months.

John's story is all too common in corporate America. His life and career were ruined as a direct result of alcoholism and addiction left untreated. What's tragic is that it could have been prevented if other people had intervened on his behalf.

Barriers to Managing Workplace Addiction[14]

- Managers and supervisors do not have enough training on how to confront employee performance problems.

- Employees who are abusing alcohol are often performing adequately on the job. This lulls managers into leaving well enough alone.

- Employees can refuse to be referred to the company-sponsored treatment program. Making it available is not the same as making it mandatory.

- Many companies are tough on illicit drugs but soft on alcohol. That's because companies don't view alcohol, which is legal and widely used, as a "drug."

- Supervisors and managers fear that they will pay a price for confronting a worker who has a problem with alcohol. No one wants to step in harm's way.

- Unions sometimes protect problem drinkers in their zealotry to protect workers' rights. On the flip side, they are strong supporters of chemical treatment and recovery programs.

- Barriers are greatest for female managers, first line supervisors, and managers in larger worksites. They can hide more easily behind the cover of anonymity.

Women employees may have a harder time seeking treatment than their male counterparts. That's because women are not supposed to have a drinking problem. It's considered unbecoming and "unladylike," so many women hide their drinking. Instead of becoming the life of the company party, like some men who drink, they fade into the woodwork. Rather than boast about worshipping the porcelain god over the weekend, they are silent on the subject of overdosing and hangovers. Their drinking sometimes goes unnoticed until it reaches a true crisis. That's what happened to Susan, a magazine editor with a quiet but ruinous drinking problem. Unlike John, she rebounded after a successful intervention by her peers.

Women in the Shadows

Susan, the publisher of an award-winning city magazine, has been in recovery for years. She explains the phenomenon of women alcoholics like this: "Being an alcoholic didn't fit my view of myself. I was well educated, successful, and highly paid. As the head of a major magazine and a dozen profitable specialty publications, I commanded a lot of respect. I saw myself as sort of a role model for other women in the field.

"I had been drinking heavily since grad school but thought I had it under control. I never missed a day of work because of drinking. And I made it a personal policy to stay out of the bars. I drank at home. I drank alone. Pretty soon, I drank all the time. I began to lose my edge. Important projects slipped through the cracks. I lost interest in the magazine and my work. My staff, and the owner of the publishing network, began to get concerned.

"Eventually, my company did an intervention. I was livid at first. It took me a long time to come to terms with my drinking. What I finally realized was that it was my behavior, not my identity, that made me an alcoholic. A few weeks into treatment, my indignation turned to relief, and eventually to gratitude. I've been clean and sober for six years now. When new employees find out that I'm a recovering alcoholic, they're always surprised. I don't look the part."

Productivity After Treatment

The destiny of an addicted employee or executive who does not get help is predictable. The only question is how fast things will unravel. The fate of an employee who does get help is full of promise. People who come back from the grave of addiction are generally so grateful for the support they received—from the company, co-workers, and family—that they throw themselves into their work, becoming models of loyalty and productivity. Attendance problems become nonissues. Attitudes improve. They surprise everyone, including themselves.

Before recovery, addicts might share a common theme song inspired by folk singer Willie Nelson: "I'm Always on My Mind." The song speaks to their narcissism. During recovery, however, they place a high value on relationships, compassion, and letting go of their obsession with self. The changes can be nothing shy of miraculous. Co-workers no longer find them complaining so much. Their supervisors approach them more eagerly.

There are thousands of stories of people, whose potential had been undercut by the disease, who soared to new heights after treatment. A computer whiz who was circling the drain before friends intervened now heads one of the most successful Internet companies in America. A nurse whose job was on the line was promoted to department head a year after her return from chemical dependency treatment. A restaurant franchisee whose tenure with the company was at risk due to his alcoholism just celebrated his thirtieth anniversary, complete with a diamond-studded pin and a banquet in his honor.

For years, addicts are reminded that they have so much

potential, and chastised for not using it. When they finally find sobriety, that potential becomes reality. People whose working and personal lives were in shambles resurrect their careers and families. They go on to become model employees and company leaders.

Productivity Gains after Treatment[15]

- 91 percent decrease in absenteeism
- 88 percent decrease in problems with supervisors
- 93 percent decrease in mistakes in work
- 97 percent decrease in on-the-job injuries
- 71 percent drop in injuries

A Call to Action

The message here is one of hope. All companies stand to benefit from the early intervention and treatment of employees with chemical addictions. To realize those gains, they need to become better informed about the disease, intervention strategies, and treatment. They need to understand where their role in the recovery process begins and ends. That's what this book is all about—preparing companies to recognize the problem of addiction, learn effective intervention techniques, and help addicted employees reclaim their lives and livelihoods. Taking action directly benefits the company, co-workers, friends, and families of those employees whose lives are nearly ruined as a result of substance addiction and abuse.

One thing is certain. To do nothing for the chemically dependent employee is a costly, shortsighted choice. Organizations can't afford to wear blinders or be reactive.

They must take ownership and action before the problem reaches crisis proportions. Early intervention offers the best prospect for a successful outcome. It puts time on the side of the corporation and provides more options and less mandates. Intervention enables the company to plan a strategy that is in everybody's best interest. Action always wins over apathy.

2

Recognizing Addiction

Concerns over costs, productivity, liability, and safety are inspiring even the most reluctant companies to look for evidence of addiction in their midst. Because of the complex nature of the disease, and the inherent denial factor, the signs can be elusive. Thankfully, there are several tools on the market to help businesspeople evaluate the level of addiction in their workplace. One is "Substance Abuse Prevention in the Workplace: An Employer's Guide."[1] This handy booklet was funded in 1998 by the Robert Wood Johnson Foundation and Mutual of Omaha to accompany Bill Moyers's award-winning PBS documentary, "Moyers on Addiction: Close to Home," which chronicles his family's journey through addiction and recovery. The guide, particularly valuable because it uses the workplace as its laboratory, describes the hallmarks of an addict. He or she

- is five times more likely to file a workers' compensation claim
- has twice as many unexcused work absences
- is late for work three times more often
- requests early dismissal twice as frequently
- is more likely to steal company property
- is five times more likely to injure himself or herself, or other workers

- causes 40 percent of all industrial accidents
- is 33 percent less productive
- incurs health care costs that average three times higher
- demonstrates marked, unexplained mood swings and often overreacts even to constructive criticism
- is seven times more likely to have recurring financial problems and potential wage garnishments

The value of this list lies not just in the statistics but in the behaviors it identifies. Missed work, frequent accidents and injuries, lagging productivity, moodiness, and difficulty in getting along—these are the warning signs of employee addiction. In my professional experience, I've found that alcoholics are more temperamental and sensitive than the general population, so they respond to everyday work issues more intensely. This makes them appear ornery or confrontational. They lack mental clarity, so they have a hard time staying on task and making good judgments. Not surprising, this fuzzy-mindedness makes them more accident-prone. Everything is interrelated.

In addition to behavioral abnormalities, there are telltale physical symptoms of workplace addiction. Morning hangovers are the most obvious. After getting blitzed the night before, employees may come to work without showering, shaving, or combing their hair, an indication that they never made it home or they slept in their clothes. Others exhibit classic signs of intoxication at work, such as slurred speech, bloodshot eyes, and an unsteady walk. Over time, addicted employees take on a bloated, pallid look, a sign of ill health. However, some addicted employees may keep up an appearance of normality for many years, even though their addiction is progressing.

Businesspeople need to recognize the symptoms and indicators of addiction in the workplace. However, they should not be used by an employer, untrained in chemical dependency detection, to diagnose the disease. Like most serious illnesses, substance abuse is complicated and life threatening. Only medical professionals trained in alcohol and drug addiction are qualified to diagnose and treat it.

Medical Recognition of the Disease

The American Medical Association (AMA) formally recognized the disease concept of alcoholism in 1956. This recognition marked a milestone in the understanding and treatment of alcoholism. From that time forward, the medical community approached the illness as a chronic disease instead of a character flaw or morality lapse. Another milestone came in June 1988, when the American Society of Addiction Medicine (ASAM) was admitted to the AMA House of Delegates as a voting member. This admission put its members on equal footing with other members of the medical community, giving credence to their work and renewed attention to the disease. Two years later, the AMA added "addiction medicine" to its list of designated specialties. These developments, while minor in the annals of medical history, have been vital to the removal of the barriers surrounding addiction. By reclassifying alcoholism as a disease, the AMA helped alter the stigma attached to alcoholism and make treatment more available to its sufferers.

In defining the illness, the ASAM observed that alcoholism mirrors many of the features attributable to other widely recognized diseases. These are listed in the sidebar "Disease Traits of Alcoholism."

Disease Traits of Alcoholism

- *Alcoholism can be described and defined.*
- *Alcoholism has a predictable progression.* It

moves through early, middle, and late stages, with definitive warning signs at each stage.

- *The loss of control over alcohol is primary to the disease.* It is not a symptom of an underlying disorder.

- *Alcoholism is permanent.* Once a person has lost control of his or her drinking, he or she will not regain it.

- *Alcoholism is terminal.* Alcoholism is directly or indirectly the cause of death for most alcoholics who do not seek treatment.

- *Alcoholism is treatable.* Total abstinence from alcohol is the necessary first step in the treatment of alcoholism. For most alcoholics, long-term, outside support also is essential for a lifetime of recovery.[2]

Despite wide acceptance of alcoholism as a disease, many physicians still are reluctant to confront the issue of alcoholism and addiction with their patients. Their discomfort is due, in part, to a legitimate lack of information and training. In many medical schools, alcoholism and drug addictions are an afterthought in the academic curriculum. Graduates aren't prepared to address the illnesses, let alone treat them. Fortunately, many reputable medical schools and treatment centers around the country are beginning to train doctors in addiction medicine. Better yet, the medical community is embracing the extensive body of research that suggests that alcoholism and drug addiction are treatable.

Symptoms of Addiction

There are five main symptoms of addiction. These symptoms can be observed at work as well as at home.

1. *Loss of control.* The primary symptom of addiction is a total loss of control of the person's use of chemicals. When an impaired employee loses control of his or her use of alcohol or drugs, willpower no longer applies. An employee cannot simply will himself or herself to stop abusing chemicals. Nor can one reason with a person who has lost control. Any reference to a previous incident of chemical abuse is meaningless, regardless of how destructive it may have been. Nothing helps at this point, short of receiving help from the outside. The popular "Just Say No" slogan coined by First Lady Nancy Reagan was a fine rallying call, but it works only for social drinkers. It has no bearing on the alcoholic or addict. If the addicted employee could just say no, he or she would have done so long before problems began to invade work and family life.

2. *Mental obsession and compulsion.* If loss of control is the primary symptom of alcoholism and addiction, mental obsession and compulsion are close seconds. They create a dangerous scenario in employees with addictions. Mental obsession is the relentless voice in the addict's head that urges him or her to drink or use, no matter what the consequences are. Obsession is the thought side of the addiction coin. Compulsion is the seemingly uncontrollable urge to use. It's the action side. Active addiction pushes addicts and alcoholics to flip between the two sides. The combination makes addicted employees feel like they have no choice but to act on their impulses. They must drink or use drugs to quiet the internal voices. Once mental obsession takes

hold, addicts feel that they have lost control over their actions. A sense of absolute powerlessness overtakes them. Their judgment is impaired, leaving them with little ability to resist temptation. They feel like they're in a dead-end maze with no escape route.

Most addicts and alcoholics are incapable of handling the one-two punch of obsession and compulsion on their own. The dynamic creates an altered perception of reality. When obsession and compulsion kick in, they don't care about anything else, regardless of how difficult and painful past consequences may have been, including getting fired. This preoccupation with alcohol or drugs can be extremely difficult for the supervisors, family, and friends to understand. Out of ignorance, they ask the addicted person why he or she continues to use. They do not understand the obsession and compulsion of addiction. The addict's destructive behavior does not make rational sense, except to other alcoholics or addicts who may have been paralyzed by the same double whammy.

3. *Denial factor.* Addiction is one of the only diseases known to medical science that tells the afflicted person that he or she doesn't have it. Like gambling and mental health problems, it's a disease of altered perceptions. The inherent denial factor is such a significant part of addiction that it figures prominently in the official definition of alcoholism that the ASAM uses:

> Alcoholism is a primary, chronic disease with genetic, psychosocial and environmental factors influencing its development and manifestation. The disease is often progressive and fatal. It is characterized by continuous or periodic impaired control over drinking, preoccupation with the drug alcohol, use of alcohol

despite adverse consequences, and distortions in thinking, most notably denial.[3]

The National Council on Alcoholism defines the denial factor as a defense mechanism that disavows the significance of events. It includes a wide range of psychological maneuvers that convince the user that alcohol is a solution to problems instead of a cause. In shorthand, the denial factor causes a serious case of self-delusion. It represents a major obstacle to recovery. Unlike most medical patients, alcoholics can't be counted on to ask for help on their own. Instead, denial drives them to engage in elaborate cover-ups and rouses, as they attempt to hide both their consumption and the negative consequences that accompany it. Classic workplace cover-up tactics include the following:

- Paying for alcohol or drugs with cash so there's no paper trail. That way, receipts turned in as part of expense reports never reveal that drinking took place.
- Lacing morning coffee with vodka or other odorless liquors.
- Stashing bottles, pills, or pipes in unlikely places—file drawers, recycling bins under the desk, or lockers—so the supply is available to satisfy any workday craving or to keep up a buzz.
- Keeping chemicals in the car for use during the morning commute or noon lunch break.
- Carrying a flask or small stash of pills in a suit pocket or purse for quick access.
- Disposing of empty bottles off premises to avoid attracting the attention of the cleaning crew or other employees.

- Getting a head start on drinking before attending after-work gatherings. This gives the appearance of "moderate consumption."
- Hitting the bars with a different group of co-workers each night, so no one notices the frequency of happy hour visits. Rotating liquor stores also keeps the tab at any one of them artificially low.
- Finding any excuse to justify a drink—welcoming a new employee, toasting a retiree, or celebrating a major new contract.

When these techniques are successful, addicts come to believe their own deception. They convince themselves that the problem is nonexistent.

4. *Euphoric recall.* People who are unfamiliar with the dynamics of this complex disease have a difficult time understanding why someone who has suffered repeatedly as a direct result of drinking or drug using cannot draw upon this negative experience to keep from repeating the behavior. The reason is simple but confounding. At the critical point of deciding to drink or use drugs, addicts recall past episodes with great pleasure. They are unable to access memories of pain, humiliation, and remorse tied to past using sprees. This phenomenon is called "euphoric recall." It makes the concept of learning from experience devoid of meaning. Addicts' memory banks are dominated by good times, warm feelings, and an absence of consequences. To them, it makes sense to drink or use.

5. *Disassociation from feelings.* Alcoholism and addiction have been called "the feelings diseases" because they shut down a person's ability to experience and be conscious of his or her own feelings. When an employee self-medicates with alcohol or drugs over a period of

time, he or she freezes up inside. When this happens, the afflicted person may not be able to access the appropriate feelings to match everyday events in life. It can appear that the employee does not have a conscience or is incapable of caring about other people. This is far from the case. Employees suffering from addiction just can't tap the appropriate reactions or responses when they need them. Their apparent lack of feelings bewilders the people who work and live with them. They may get the reputation of an S.O.B. who's impossible to work for or with.

Frozen Feelings

From the outside, Jerry seemed like the Mr. Nice Guy. He and his wife owned a small print shop that had a reputation for supporting community causes. He spent his free time coaching girls' soccer, serving as a volunteer firefighter, and carting his three young daughters to practices, dance lessons, and church activities.

To his family and employees, however, Jerry looked more like Mr. Ice Man. While he showed concern for outside causes, he was becoming increasingly blind to the internal needs of his staff and customers. He blew off employee concerns about unsafe equipment as quickly as he did customer complaints about shoddy quality and missed deadlines. When a longtime employee approached him for time off to move his ailing parents to a nursing home, he shooed him away without a word of condolence. When his bindery man lost a finger in a work-related accident, he didn't even bother to send a card. Word in the shop was that Jerry didn't give a damn about anything but his kids and his causes.

Although he adored his kids, Jerry was growing more distant from them as they grew older. He frequently missed family dinners, claiming that he had a committee meeting or firefighter training session after work. In fact, he was slipping off to the local watering hole. He skipped soccer practices with regularity for the same reason. The last straw was when he missed his youngest daughter's first dance recital. He'd stopped for a beer on the way to the recital and never showed up. She was crushed, thinking that her daddy didn't love her anymore. He was unfazed, lamely promising to catch next year's recital while plunking down in front of the TV with a brew and the remote control.

Jerry's wife was livid, in part because he hadn't shown up, but mostly because he didn't seem to be bothered by his actions. She knew that he loved their girls, but was baffled by his behavior. It was so out of character for this otherwise caring man. She'd heard their staff voice the same concerns. How could such a nice guy be so unfeeling?

His wife went to a counselor to find out. The answer was that Jerry had been self-medicating with alcohol for so long that he had disassociated himself from his own feelings. He still had the capacity to feel compassion, remorse, or empathy, but he couldn't access his feelings. They were numbed by the drug. The counselor explained that this disassociation from feelings was common among people with addictions. Because it disguises itself as callousness or insensitivity, disassociation causes great confusion among family, friends, and co-workers. It's the addict's inability to express appropriate emotion that often pushes family members to seek treatment for them.

Archetype of the Addict or Alcoholic

Human resource managers and employee assistance professionals face a daunting challenge. They are the people most often charged with identifying and helping employees tormented by addiction. But beyond the behavioral and physical hallmarks just described, there are no standard profiles of a substance abuser. The typical user is someone in his or her midforties who holds a responsible job and is raising a family. That could be anybody. Fewer than 5 percent of all alcoholics fit the destitute image portrayed in movies and books. The majority blend into the ranks of the workforce. They could be the controller, the president, or the night janitor. That's because alcoholism is completely nondiscriminatory. It gives no regard to organizational charts, pay scales, or resumés. It afflicts both sexes and all ethnic, religious, economic, and affinity groups.

Alcoholic archetypes simply don't exist; however, drinking is more imbedded in the culture of some workplaces, professions, and industries. It's all but absent from others. The Department of Health and Human Services found that construction, hospitality, warehousing, and sales ranked higher in their incidence of substance abuse—including alcohol and illicit drugs—than other industries.[4] It stands to reason. In the hospitality industry, promoting drinking helps the bottom line. In sales, drinking is believed to be an important part of courting a client or closing a deal. Table 2–1 lists occupations with high drug and alcohol use.

Professional sports and entertainment rank high on the addiction scale as well. These are high-stakes industries that attract people who are willing to bet all on a chance for glory. Caution and restraint are not part of the mindset. Like many high achievers, some athletes and performers are afflicted with a case of "terminal uniqueness." That's my shorthand for the belief system that says rules don't apply to them. They believe that they are exceptions—to the biology of addiction, the laws of the land, and the rules of propriety.

The face of addiction varies widely by profession. For example, only a fraction of female librarians are affected by alcohol abuse, while close to half of all male bartenders have drinking problems. It stands to reason that constant exposure to a drinking environment encourages use. And of the people who use, almost 20 percent will develop a drinking problem. Numerous statistics confirm the reality.

Abuse hits members of other professions as well. The bottle can be a common companion in the high-pressure world of Wall Street or the demanding lives of doctors, lawyers, and accountants. While these people are just as vulnerable to addiction as anyone, they have more difficulty asking for help. That's because they have professional images to protect and more to lose if they are "discovered." It's also harder for them to admit that they're needy when they're used to being the ones who are needed. As a result, their illnesses go untreated longer, often becoming life threatening.

On the street, some professional-level alcoholics are called "high-bottom drunks." They are more likely to die from delayed treatment than so-called "low-bottom drunks." Professionals can hide their disease well, often too well. Unlike the most desperate and destitute of alcoholics, professionals with serious drinking problems are more likely to commit suicide. The head of a Los Angeles mission that houses skid row alcoholics describes the phenomenon this way: "We have plenty of death here, but we don't have suicide. A guy might kill for a bottle or fall in front of a bus, but he rarely takes his own life. All the suicides in this city are in Bel Aire, Beverly Hills, or Hollywood Hills, where folks have money. The people here have already given up. They don't have anything left to lose."

Many professionals see themselves as safe from the grasp of addiction because they tend to be well educated and highly paid. Not true. Neither college degrees nor six-digit incomes provide immunity from drug or alcohol addiction. They're used to thinking of themselves as caregivers or problem solvers, not as people who need help. In many cases, they also are bosses—not easily challenged or confronted by subordinates. These professionals are slow to recognize when they have lost control.

Peer-to-peer support groups help some professionals overcome the delusions that impede recovery. Lawyers Concerned for Lawyers pairs recovering attorneys with colleagues in trouble. Physicians Concerned for Physicians provides the same service. The peer approach is effective because it places both parties on equal footings. Empathy and trust are more readily established when people share similar backgrounds and professional experiences.

While there are as many women as men who are alcoholics, workplace tolerance for drinking can be greatly influenced by gender. Male-dominated occupations tend to have a higher propensity toward heavy drinking and alcoholism than female-dominated occupations. Part of the reason is men's greater need to be accepted by their peers. Despite the strides toward gender equality in the last half century, social etiquette still discourages women from indulging publicly to the same extent as men. This subtle social pressure makes their drinking habits more furtive.

Table 2-1: Occupations with High Drug and Alcohol Use[5]

OCCUPATION	ILLICIT DRUG USE	ALCOHOL USE
Construction workers	15.6%	17.6%
Sales personnel	11.4%	8.3%
Food preparers, wait staff, and bartenders	11.2%	12.2%

OCCUPATION	ILLICIT DRUG USE	ALCOHOL USE
Handlers, helpers, and laborers	10.6%	15.7%
Machine operators and inspectors	10.5%	13.5%
Transportation and material movers	5.3%	13.1%
Precision production and repair workers	7.9%	13.1%

The Line between Social Drinking and Addiction

The distinction between alcoholism and social drinking is critical to any meaningful discussion of addiction. In simple terms, social drinkers use alcohol in moderation and without negative consequences. They may drink regularly, but rarely to excess and not to satisfy a need or habit. More important, drinking does not interfere with other areas of their lives. Employees who drink but are not dependent upon alcohol can stop using on demand without altering their work or personal lives.

In contrast, employees who are dependent upon alcohol cannot stop using on demand without dramatically altering their lives. Alcoholics consistently overuse alcohol, much to their detriment. Their repeated use ultimately causes trouble in every aspect of their personal, professional, and family lives. When they drink, they can't predict when they'll stop, how much they'll consume, or what the consequences will be. Their abuse, by definition, is "chronic, progressive, and potentially fatal." These employees have three choices:

1. They can continue to drink or take drugs, just as other sick people take medicine to feel better. However, sooner or later, the "cure" will kill them.

2. They can get into a treatment or recovery program like Alcoholic Anonymous (AA). Twelve Step programs are effective medicine for many people, but even they can't provide a permanent cure. They arrest the disease "one day at a time."
3. They can put the plug in the jug and stop cold turkey. This white-knuckle endurance contest works for a few, but often solves the alcohol problem without treating the alcoholism. The survivor is called a "dry drunk."

Although addiction begins with the voluntary act of drinking or taking drugs, repetition eventually changes drinking into an involuntary act. Ultimately, the behavior is driven by a compulsive craving for the alcohol or drug.[6] This compulsion stems from a combination of factors, one of which is the way that alcoholics metabolize alcohol. Another is the dramatic change in brain function produced by prolonged drinking or drug use. This helps to explain why addiction is considered "a disease of the brain."[7] Once addicted, most people find it impossible to halt the spiraling cycle on their own. They need outside professional help.

Addicts and alcoholics simply are wired differently than nonaddicts, making them more prone to addictive behavior. Often described as restless, irritable, and discontented when sober, they drink to feel more "normal," using alcohol or drugs as a form of self-medication. For them, having alcoholic tendencies is akin to being born with an allergy to ragweed. Susceptibility doesn't mean that they *will* suffer allergic symptoms, only that they are *more vulnerable* to them.

One of the major differences between social drinkers and alcoholics is the way they view alcohol. For a social drinker, alcohol is a beverage. For an alcoholic, it's a medicine. The issue is not what alcohol does *to* the alcoholic, but what it does *for* the alcoholic. Recovering alcoholics and addicts often say that they had to use chemicals just to get through the day. A feeling of emptiness or rejection plagues many until they take chemicals. Alcohol and drugs are the salve that makes the wound stop hurting, at least temporarily.

Some people drink or use chemicals to relieve stress. Others use alcohol to feel better when they are depressed or experiencing difficulties in life. For many, what starts as a solution ends up creating an even larger problem. Once this dependency bridge is crossed, excessive drinkers have little chance of effectively dealing with their life issues until they resolve their substance abuse. Counseling is of little benefit, because the disease masks true feelings and rational reasoning. Out of respect for their time and mine, I often discontinue therapy with people who refuse to deal with active addiction head-on. It's counterproductive.

The challenge of identifying addictive behavior magnifies when an employee's chemical use shifts from recreational to abusive. Because addiction is a process, people don't just "get alcoholism" like they get a virus. They often slip into it over time, making the task of pinpointing the change a difficult one. The best advice for an employer concerned about an employee's addiction is to base all of his or her judgments on observable changes in work performance and on-the-job behavior. Compare past behavior to current behavior, focusing on the degree and scope of change. Narrowing initial observations to work-related issues makes it easier to recognize emerging patterns of abuse.

Substance abuse at work erodes ambition, efficiency, or both. When a weekend drinker becomes a weekday drinker, he or she is less alert on the job, struggles with stifled creativity, or is less communicative with other employees. The employee may come in hung over, decline opportunities to take on visible projects, or botch even routine tasks. The patterns may go unnoticed for a while, until all of a sudden they capture the attention of other employees. Rarely are these changes visible to the abuser.

What about the alcoholic who never misses a day of work, or consistently does a good job, while secretly harboring an addiction? This poses a dilemma for the employer. On the one hand, it's hard to justify an intervention if there are no apparent symptoms. On the other hand, the workplace is usually the last place that addiction reveals itself. Home is the first place. Holding down a job does not prove that someone is addiction-free, only that he or she places a high priority on work. As a practical matter, job wages are needed to support a habit. As a psychological matter, work is a source of self-respect, one that many addicts protect at all costs. They even point to the fact that they make it to work every day as reassurance that they don't have a problem. With this said, an employer's decision to get involved should be based on measurable performance standards. If the employee were meeting the standards of the job, the employer would be out of line to intervene—unless requested to do so by the employee's family.

Slipping into Addiction

The sales manager at a Detroit-based Jeep dealership was disturbed about Joleen, his top salesperson. After posting record sales for three years straight, Joleen seemed to have lost her touch. Her average sales dropped from twenty-five vehicles a month to half that number, despite a robust economy and strong numbers from the rest of the sales force. Once a model of efficiency, she routinely showed up late for weekly sales meetings, blundered the paperwork for her deliveries, and forgot customer appointments. Twice he found her napping in her car after lunch.

He started to pay closer attention. Joleen had been a congenial person who seemed to get along with anyone. Lately, she was in frequent conflict with the detailing department and had fueled the ire of other reps with offhand remarks and accusations. She seemed moody and irritable. Her behavior was driving even her regular customers to other dealerships.

The sales manager was concerned that the change in Joleen's performance and demeanor might be triggered by a medical condition or family crisis. He also suspected drugs or alcohol. He decided to document what he observed and take the matter to the dealership's personnel department for direction and options on intervention, even though the circumstances might not be attributable to addiction.

On-the-Job Substance Use

Contrary to conventional wisdom, most substance abuse isn't limited to after-work use. In interviews with employees who sought help for addiction,[8] most admitted to using drugs on the job. They acknowledged that their performance suffered because of it. Almost half said that they had sold drugs to other employees. This helps explain how addiction can spread through an organization. A smaller number of those interviewed admitted to stealing from their employers or co-workers. Sometimes it was their stealing that triggered an intervention. Other times, it was their anomalous behavior, as in Joleen's case described earlier. Either way, something eventually blew their cover. The effects of substance abuse are difficult to

keep under wraps. One exception is workplace marijuana usage. It can be harder to detect than workplace
drinking, and for that reason, harder to treat. Pot makes
users appear mellow and agreeable, so they fade into the
shadows more readily. The behavioral effects are subtle
and hard to recognize.

While the signs of drinking can be hard to disguise,
the act of drinking itself is not. Most workplace drinkers
find it very easy to bring alcohol to work, to drink at their
workstations, and to tip a few brews on breaks. Managers
either don't see the activity or opt to ignore it. Co-workers
and friends may see it, but won't report it out of loyalty or
a misguided attempt to protect the offending employee.
Some shy away to avoid a potential backlash. In not taking action, friends, co-workers, and supervisors give tacit
approval to the practice of workplace drinking. That
makes them part of the problem. They are what addiction literature calls "enablers." They can't seem to think
beyond their immediate discomfort with the situation to
consider the long-term impact of substance abuse in their
midst. They foster an environment where on-the-job
drinking is permissible.

Patterns of Use and Abuse

In this era of heightened sensitivity about workplace
drinking and drug use, it's important to remember that
not every incident involving alcohol heralds an addiction. If this were so, most of the workforce would be in
company-sponsored treatment programs. Just because an
employee has an isolated incident associated with chemical use does not make him or her an addict. Addiction experts search for patterns of use, among other things, when
assessing employee substance abuse. They also look for
reoccurring consequences resulting from the use. When

use causes a series of negative consequences, rather than a single backlash, there's reason to suspect the presence of alcoholism. In other words, not all use is abuse, and not all abuse is addiction.

Lapse of Judgment

Mike is a married father of three and works as a production manager for a wicker furniture manufacturer and distributor in North Carolina. His boss required him to have an independent chemical dependency evaluation in 1998, following a work-related incident involving alcohol. He had received a ticket for driving under the influence (DUI) while heading home from a late-night furniture showcase in a company vehicle. Everyone, including Mike, was concerned about the event.

His first comment after leaving the police station was how lucky he felt not to have hurt anyone while behind the wheel. He understood that his actions could have permanently changed his life and the lives of others on the road. He acknowledged that he should have curtailed his drinking or turned the vehicle over to a designated driver who was not drinking. Either decision would have prevented the mishap.

Mike's wife participated in his assessment. Her presence provided a valuable outside perspective on his alcohol use. The chemical dependency counselor looked for other incidents or consequences in his past that were related to alcohol or drug use. Although he'd been drinking alcohol since high school, Mike did not appear to have any kind of problems directly associated with chemicals. His drinking had not affected any other major areas of his life—most notably health, finances, or relationships.

Mike had made one bad decision and was suffering the consequences—one of which was undergoing a chemical dependency assessment. He did not minimize or deny his actions, a common response among people with chronic drinking problems. Instead, he exhibited a real sense of responsibility and remorse. There was no pattern of repetition or alcohol-related dysfunction in his work or home life. The counselor determined that Mike was not chemically dependent.

Alcoholism doesn't fit into a tidy box. It manifests itself in at least four different stages, depending on the person and the progression of the disease. First, it starts with *experimentation*, which usually doesn't reveal itself at work and by itself does not constitute an addiction. It then advances to *recreational use*, which might include having a beer at lunch or a pitcher with the company bowling league. Employees at this stage use alcohol to feel different or fit in. This kind of drinking is considered acceptable in most business circles. It describes Mike's drinking habits. The biggest risk of recreational drinking is that it sets up the person for the third stage, *dependency*.

Dependency is considered mid-addiction. It's elusive, because dependent employees appear to be in control even though a drug is running their lives. They lose their ability to choose, relying instead upon the chemical to cope, to relax, to feel good, or to perform. They avoid places where they can't use, or they use before or after work. This is the stage when employees start to compromise their principles to support their habit. An example is the CPA who "borrows" $5,000 of her client's money to fund her habit, violating both personal and professional codes of ethics. Employees in this stage are among the walking wounded. That's where Joleen fits in. They can't save themselves, but they can be rescued through intervention. This stage accounts for an increasingly larger percent of workplace interventions.

The fourth stage is full-blown *addiction*. Chemicals

have become the top priority in life, overriding work, family, health, and self-respect. Addicted employees go to extreme measures to get and use drugs. They are powerless over their behavior, driven by an uncontrollable craving, which must be satisfied at all costs. In many cases, alcohol abuse has to escalate to this level before co-workers or family members recognize the symptoms and feel compelled to act. This belated reaction is unfortunate, because the earlier addiction is arrested through intervention and treatment, the better the chances for recovery. Left unchecked, it is eventually fatal.

Death from untreated addiction is as difficult to document as the symptoms of the disease itself. It robs the body of health, causing a slow and painful deterioration that's hard to detect. People rarely see it coming. When alcoholism claims a victim, the obituary usually lists liver failure, heart attack, pneumonia, or car accident as the cause. In reality, these are merely symptoms. Even though the public overlooks the fatal nature of addiction, the official death toll is hard to ignore. In the United States alone, alcoholism contributes to hundreds of thousands of deaths each year.[9]

The Line between Dependency and Abuse

The Diagnostic and Statistical Manual of Mental Disorders (DSM IV) further distinguishes between "substance dependency" and "substance abuse," the two major stages of addiction affecting the workplace. Counselors and addiction professionals use the DSM IV's Substance Dependence Criteria to assess the severity of an employee's addiction and to develop an appropriate treatment plan. The abbreviated criteria listed below are not intended to turn businesspeople into instant addiction experts. They're included only as a simple barometer of addiction in the workplace.

According to the DSM IV,[10] an employee is likely to be "dependent" if he or she exhibits *three or more* of the following within a year's time:

- *Increased tolerance.* This is defined as either a need for much greater amounts of a substance to get the same buzz, or a much lower effect from taking the same dose.
- *Withdrawal.* This includes characteristic symptoms like uncontrollable shakes, fevers, and sweats. It also includes use of the same or a similar substance to relieve or avoid withdrawal symptoms.
- *Escalating use.* Employees continue to take the substance in larger amounts or over a longer period than was intended.
- *Desire to reduce use.* The employee wants to cut down on his or her use, or has repeatedly tried to cut down without success.
- *Time-consuming.* The employee spends a great deal of time getting the substance, using it, or recovering from its effects.
- *Missed opportunities.* Important work, social, or recreational activities are given up or reduced because of the substance.
- *Continued use.* The employee continues to use the substance despite persistent or recurrent physical or psychological problems that are exacerbated by the substance. For example, he or she continues to use cocaine despite knowing that it increases the risk of a heart attack, or continues to drink despite knowing that alcohol aggravates an ulcer.

The following shorthand criteria, also adapted from the DSM IV, can help employers determine if an employee's use has escalated to abuse. The user needs to meet *only one* of the following over the course of a year to qualify as a substance "abuser":

- *Failure to meet obligations.* Recurrent use results in failure to meet major obligations at work or home.
- *High-risk or hazardous use.* The employee continues to use in situations that are physically hazardous, as in driving a car or operating a machine.
- *Recurrent problems.* These may include arrests for substance-related assaults at work and lawsuits over drug-induced harassment.
- *Interpersonal problems.* The employee continues to use despite persistent social or interpersonal problems.

Linking Behaviors and Consequences

While it's helpful to recognize the behaviors associated with employee addiction, it's sometimes more instructive to look at the work-related consequences of those behaviors—especially as they change with the progression of the disease. What starts as a productivity problem can spiral into more serious issues if employee addiction spreads through an organization. The four phases in table 2-2, developed by New Beginnings Treatment Center and used by clinicians all over the country, tracks the manifold consequences of addiction. Comprehensive and compact, it belongs on the bulletin board of every small business owner and HR staff member in America. The chart addresses the impact of alcoholism on home life as well as work life, since what happens after hours directly impacts on-the-job performance. When an afflicted employee's spouse moves out because conditions at home become unsafe or intolerable, the employee often will bring the emotional carnage of separation into the workplace. When evenings are interrupted by creditor calls and money worries, employees come to work distracted and unable to focus at work. Productivity plummets, emotions rage. Co-workers can't escape the fallout. Addiction is like a Kansas tornado, with the addict in the eye of the storm. Anything that happens to be in its path of destruction—including family, friends, and co-workers—is at risk. The first defense is early detection. That's what the chart on the next two pages helps employers do. The second defense is immediate action, often through intervention.

Table 2-2: Four Phases of Addictive Behaviors[11]

Early Phase One		
Behaviors	*Visible Signs*	*Consequences*
• Alcohol tolerance increases • Blackouts • Lies about drinking • Drinks to relieve tension	• Attendance problems • Late after lunch, more critical of other employees • Leaves work early • Absent from office • Fellow workers complain • Overreacts to real or imagined criticism • Complains of not feeling well • Lies • Misses deadlines • Mistakes through inattention or poor judgment • Decreased efficiency	• Criticism from supervisor • Attitude begins to change at work • More critical of other employees
Phase Two		
Behaviors	*Visible Signs*	*Consequences*
• Guilt about drinking • Tremors during hangovers • Loss of interest	• Frequent days off for vague ailments or implausible reasons • Statements become undependable • Begins to avoid associates • Borrows money from co-workers • Exaggerates work accomplishments • Hospitalized more than normal • Repeated minor injuries on and off job • Unreasonable resentments • General deterioration in job performance • Attention wanders, difficulty focusing	• Family problems • Loss of job advancement • Financial problems • Warning from boss

Used with permission of New Beginnings Treatment Center, Waverly, Minnesota.

Phase Three

Behaviors	Visible Signs	Consequences
• Avoids discussion of problem • Fails in efforts to control • Neglects food (poor eating habits) • Prefers to drink alone	• Frequent time off, sometimes for several days • Fails to return from lunch • Grandiose, aggressive behavior among men and passive, withdrawn behavior among women • Domestic problems interfere with work • Apparent loss of ethical values • Money problems, garnishment of wages • Hospitalization increase • Refuses to discuss problem • Trouble with the law • Job performance far below expectations	• Trouble with the law • Punitive disciplinary actions taken • Serious family problems, separation

Phase Four

Behaviors	Visible Signs	Consequences
• Believes that other activities are interfering with his/her drinking • Hallucinations • Severe withdrawal symptoms when not drinking everyday	• Prolonged, unpredictable absences • Drinking on the job • Totally undependable • Repeated hospitalization • Physical deterioration • Money problems worsen • Separation or divorce • Uneven and incompetent job performance	• Final warning from boss • Area of greatest cover up • Most serious financial problems, bankruptcy • Hospitalization • Termination from job

The Progressive Nature of Addiction

Medical science still has a lot to learn about alcoholism and addiction, but this much is true: Addiction is progressive. Left untreated, it gets worse, not better. For employers, this means the problem will not correct itself on its own. It also means employers should not put much stock in employees' claims that they can remedy their addiction on their own. If addiction were that easy to treat, millions of people wouldn't be debilitated by it each year.

Substance abuse professionals struggle with how to estimate the exact rate of progression—meaning how fast an employee will deteriorate after diagnosis. The rate varies greatly from one individual to the next. Even when armed with family histories, psychological testing, chemical health histories, and other relevant information, professionals are hard pressed to predict the pace of decline. Figure 2-1 is a chart developed by Dr. Elvin M. Jellinek, a pioneer in the field of addiction and recovery research. The chart depicts the downward spiral of addiction. The "Jellinek Chart," as it's known in clinical circles, is as relevant today as the day it made addiction medical news in the 1950s.

Figure 2-1: Phases of Alcohol Addiction[12]

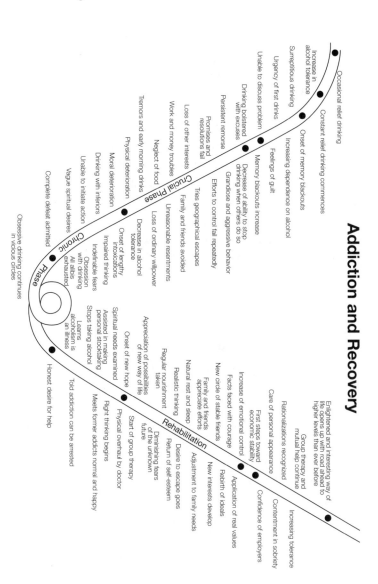

Addiction and Recovery

Occasional relief drinking

Constant relief drinking commences

Increase in alcohol tolerance

Surreptitious drinking

Onset of memory blackouts

Increasing dependence on alcohol

Urgency of first drinks

Unable to discuss problem

Feelings of guilt

Drinking bolstered with excuses

Memory blackouts increase

Decrease of ability to stop drinking when others do so

Persistent remorse

Grandiose and aggressive behavior

Promises and resolutions fail

Efforts to control fail repeatedly

Loss of other interests

Tries geographical escapes

Work and money troubles

Family and friends avoided

Neglect of food

Unreasonable resentments

Tremors and early morning drinks

Loss of ordinary willpower

Physical deterioration

Decrease in alcohol tolerance

Moral deterioration

Onset of lengthy intoxications

Drinking with inferiors

Impaired thinking

Unable to initiate action

Indefinable fears

Obsession with drinking

Vague spiritual desires

All alibis exhausted

Complete defeat admitted

Crucial Phase

Chronic Phase

Obsessive drinking continues in vicious circles

Learns alcoholism is an illness

Stops taking alcohol

Honest desire for help

Told addiction can be arrested

Meets former addicts normal and happy

Right thinking begins

Assisted in making personal stocktaking

Physical overhaul by doctor

Spiritual needs examined

Start of group therapy

Onset of new hope

Diminishing fears of the unknown future

Appreciation of possibilities of new way of life

Desire to escape goes

Regular nourishment taken

Return of self-esteem

Realistic thinking

Adjustment to family needs

Natural rest and sleep

New interests develop

Family and friends appreciate efforts

Rebirth of ideals

New circle of stable friends

Application of real values

Facts faced with courage

Increase of emotional control

Confidence of employers

First steps toward economic stability

Care of personal appearance

Contentment in sobriety

Rationalizations recognized

Increasing tolerance

Group therapy and mutual help continue

Enlightened and interesting way of life opens up with road ahead to higher levels than ever before

Rehabilitation

Downward Spiral

Juanita was a district manager in her midthirties. She'd been working full-time for a gift collectibles company for six years. She was outgoing and dependable, had a strong work record, and led a seemingly normal family life. When her behavior became erratic and unpredictable, it threw her employer and her family into a panic. Alcohol was the suspected culprit. After ruling out other possible causes, they called in a professional alcohol interventionist. To unearth the root cause of her errant behavior, the interventionist interviewed her family, co-workers, and boss. He discovered a demonstrated inability to control her drinking, dating back at least a decade. The problem had reached a crisis all at once, catching even those who knew her well off-guard.

Her parents reported being concerned over her heavy drinking as early as her college years. Yet, as often is the case, they had refrained from taking action in the early stages. They mentioned that in recent months, their daughter had begun to isolate herself, miss family functions, and not return telephone calls. This reclusive behavior was out of character and a source of great consternation.

Juanita's boss had not detected any drinking problem until she began missing work with frequency. She also took longer lunch breaks, sometimes returning with alcohol on her breath. Her work performance declined, prompting her boss to contact her family and initiate an intervention.

Once confronted, Juanita seemed surprised that people were concerned about her. In her state of altered perception, she believed that she was doing fine. After all, she'd been able to manage her life and her drinking for more than ten years without complications. This was the demon denial talking. It was not until she went into treatment and got sober that she could see how much alcoholism had warped her life.

On her one-year anniversary of sobriety, she approached her family and co-workers to thank them for intervening and saving her from self-destruction.

When the disease begins to progress, changes are noticeable in at least five major areas—physical health, drinking patterns and behaviors, blackouts, reversed intolerance, and emotional well-being. These changes can cause distress and confusion, even to the person who is using. Take the instance of reversed tolerance. An employee who may be able to down a case of beer in one sitting becomes completely intoxicated on one or two drinks the next. After years of drinking, he can no longer predict his body's response to the drug. This strange phenomenon is a late-stage symptom. It results from a physiological change in the way the body metabolizes alcohol.

Employers are often surprised to learn that addiction continues to progress even after an employee maintains complete abstinence. An employee can remain clean and sober for years, but when he or she begins to drink alcohol again, the illness leapfrogs ahead. Consumption levels quickly move from moderation to excess, progressing far beyond where they had been before recovery. Sometimes, after years of slow progression, the disease will pick up speed at a rapid clip. This acceleration can be fueled by a life-changing event, such as a job layoff, divorce, or death in the family. It also can happen for no apparent reason. That's the confounding nature of addiction. Recovery is a temporary state between active drinking and rapid demise. It holds only as long as abstinence rules.

The Complacency Delusion

Bill, a thirty-year veteran of the medical device industry, worked for several start-ups before landing the job of shop foreman for a California-based heart valve manufacturer. As a young man, he drank heavily and suffered the consequences that follow addiction. He finally sought treatment for chemical dependency and launched a twenty-five-year commitment to sobriety.

In recent years, complacency began to set in. Bill stopped attending Alcoholics Anonymous meetings, convincing himself that he didn't need the support after so many years of abstinence. Although alcoholism never gets "cured," he started to believe that he had beaten it, that he was not an alcoholic anymore. The disease played tricks on his psyche. It told him that he could drink again, without any negative consequences, if he just kept it under control. He became delusional, reassuring himself that even if he did experience problems from drinking again, they would be a long way off. He thought he had a reprieve from the negative consequences of addiction, due to his long-term sobriety.

Once Bill started drinking again, he surpassed where he had left off twenty-five years before within a few weeks. It wasn't long before drinking dominated his life again. His wife tried to talk to him about his drinking, but with no success. The plant manager also was stonewalled in his attempt to get Bill help. He soon lost his wife, his job, and his self-respect.

Long-term sobriety provides no more protection against the effects of recurring alcoholism than long-term suntanning protects against skin cancer. Complacency puts recovering addicts at great risk.

People are perplexed by the notion that employees who are in recovery from alcoholism or addiction need to continue in a Twelve Step program even after they have stopped using chemicals. The explanation is imbedded in the nature of addiction. Recovering addicts are potentially powerless over the obsession and compulsion of the addiction. They are inherently unable to counteract the complex dynamics of addiction—especially over an extended period of time, and on their own. The single greatest factor associated with relapse is isolation from support mechanisms. Recovering alcoholics and addicts who attempt to manage and treat their illness without outside support fail at a distressingly high rate. An estimated 75 percent experience at least one relapse.

A Clinical Framework for Assessing Alcoholism

Alcoholism and drug addictions are complex illnesses. To help businesspeople make sense of the conundrum, it's helpful to review the clinical framework that has been developed to assess the diseases. Again, the intent here is not to make sales managers and shop stewards into addiction diagnosticians, but to give them a clear sense of what addiction looks like in the workplace. Their goal is to watch for icebergs of addiction before the corporate ship steers into one and to send out an early call for help while there's still time to react. Addicted employees can't be relied upon to flag their own addictions.

One of the most widely used diagnostic tools in the field of addiction is the famous "Twenty Questions." It was developed by Johns Hopkins Medical School to help evaluate whether or not a patient is alcoholic. This basic litmus test helps gauge the severity of an employee's potential substance abuse problem. While highly respected in medical circles, its standard for assessing addiction tends to be rigid and unforgiving. Sensitivity and expertise are called for in interpreting the results. It's only one set of criteria that counselors and addiction professions use when assessing alcoholism.

Are You an Alcoholic?[13]

To answer this questionnaire, ask yourself the following questions and answer them as honestly as you can:

1. Do you lose time from work due to drinking?
2. Is drinking making your home life unhappy?
3. Do you drink because you are shy with other people?
4. Is drinking affecting your reputation?
5. Have you ever felt remorse after drinking?
6. Have you gotten into financial difficulties as a result of drinking?
7. Do you turn to lower companions and an inferior environment when drinking?
8. Does your drinking make you careless of your family's welfare?
9. Has your ambition decreased since drinking?
10. Do you crave a drink at a definite time daily?
11. Do you want a drink the next morning?
12. Does drinking cause you to have difficulty in sleeping?
13. Has your efficiency decreased since drinking?
14. Is drinking jeopardizing your job or business?
15. Do you drink to escape from worries or trouble?
16. Do you drink alone?
17. Have you ever had a complete loss of memory as a result of drinking?
18. Has your physician ever treated you for drinking?
19. Do you drink to build up your self-confidence?
20. Have you ever been to a hospital or institution on account of drinking?

If you answered YES to any one of the questions, there is a definite warning that you may be alcoholic. If you answered YES to any two of the questions, chances are that you are an alcoholic. If you answered YES to three or more, you are definitely an alcoholic.

3

The Intervention Process

When an employee shows signs of alcoholism or addiction at work, managers face a difficult dilemma. They know they should do something, but they rarely know where to begin. Their first impulse often is to rid themselves of the problem—either by firing the employee or by initiating a transfer to another department or division. Many managers are inclined to wait on the sidelines in hopes that the problem corrects itself. A few fall into the "personal responsibility camp," which places the employee in charge of recognizing and healing his or her own addiction. Still others try to break the cycle of chemical abuse by getting the employee to promise to quit. None of these options have good prospects for success.

Dismissing an addicted employee without attempting to get him or her help is a shortsighted and punitive response, one that may expose companies to a snare of legal problems. It's ill-advised under all but the most extreme circumstances. On the other hand, waiting for alcoholism to go away on its own is folly. The progressive nature of the disease makes "spontaneous correction" an impossibility. Left untreated, addiction always gets worse, not better. And while there are instances when an employee will ask for help on his or her own, this is rare. Denial makes an addict unable to recognize his or her own addiction. The most promising solution is a combination of intervention, treatment, and lifelong maintenance.

The Mystery of Intervention

Although intervention has been used to halt the spinning wheels of addiction for more than three decades, it's still shrouded in mystery. One of the reasons is that intervention challenges the popular notion that treatment can't be effective until the addict hits rock bottom, meaning the addict has to lose everything and ask for help on his or her own. This presumption is a myth. Nothing in the collective addiction research supports the idea that employees in the throws of the disease, consumed by denial, will suddenly see the light on their own and seek help. Nor does research validate the idea that an employee must bottom out before he or she can be successful in treatment. In fact, the opposite is true. The earlier an employee gets into treatment, the less the symptoms advance—and the better the chances for recovery. Treating addiction is akin to treating other serious diseases. Early detection and treatment greatly improve the prospects for survival. While the disease is incurable, it can be put into remission.

In the early days of intervention, some clinicians believed that the only way to get impaired employees into treatment was through force. Their approach tended to be heavy-handed and confrontational. It was designed to make a bad person good, instead of a sick person well. Shame and guilt were the preferred methods of persuasion. This coercive approach created a psychological barrier in treatment that distracted the employee from getting better. Today, respect and dignity characterize the intervention process. Employees who can enter treatment without the emotional baggage of anger and shame triggered by an intervention can more quickly engage in the treatment process.

Most managers feel uncomfortable in confronting employees about their addictions. They see "intervening" as "interfering" and aren't sure where to draw the line between corporate responsibility and personal privacy. The answer is simple. When personal addiction affects workplace performance, it becomes a corporate issue. Some managers shy away from confronting employees because they don't want to incur their wrath. Avoidance only fuels the crisis. Once the employee gets treatment, heartfelt appreciation often displaces any lingering resentment about being intervened.

Ten Myths of Intervention

1. Alcoholics and addicts must hit rock bottom before getting help.
2. Alcoholics and addicts must ask for help on their own.
3. It is not okay to confront people about their alcoholism or addiction.
4. Alcoholics and addicts have a good chance of quitting on their own.
5. Unless alcoholics or addicts enter treatment on their own, the treatment will not be successful.
6. The intervention process must be heavy-handed and confrontational.
7. A person who has been intervened will resent those who participated in their intervention.
8. Guilt and shame are effective motivators to recovery.
9. The intervention model is one-size-fits-all.
10. The only person who benefits from a corporate intervention is the addicted employee.

The following anonymous letter is widely circulated among recovering addicts and their families. Written from the alcoholic's painful and powerless perspective, it highlights the importance of early intervention. In the letter, he asks those he works and lives with not to cover up the consequences of his addiction, run away from reality, or simply do nothing in an effort to avoid crisis or conflict. It calls for action. The sooner they act, the more options they have. The longer they delay, the closer they all come to smoldering coals of addiction—an auto accident on the way home from work, a physical confrontation in the warehouse, or a chemical-related accident that injures innocent employees.

An Alcoholic's Open Letter

To my Friends, Family, and Co-workers,

I am an alcoholic and I need help. Don't allow me to lie to you and accept it for the truth. For in so doing, you encourage me to lie. The truth may be painful, but get at it. Don't let me outsmart you. This only teaches me to avoid responsibility and to lose respect for you at the same time. Don't let me exploit you or take advantage of you. In so doing, you become an accomplice to my evasion of responsibility. Don't lecture me or argue with me when I am intoxicated. And don't pour out my liquor. You may feel better, but the situation will be worse. Don't accept my promises. This is only my method of postponing pain. And don't keep switching agreements. If an agreement is made, stick to it. Don't lose your temper with me. It will destroy you, and any possibility of you helping me. Don't allow your anxiety for me compel you to do what I must do for myself. Don't cover up or abort the consequences of my drinking. It reduces the crisis, but perpetuates the illness. Above all, don't run away from

reality as I do. Alcoholism, my illness, gets worse as my
drinking continues. Start now to learn, to understand,
and to plan for my recovery. I need help from a doctor,
psychologist, and other recovering alcoholics like me. I
cannot help myself. I hate myself, but I care about you. To
do nothing is the worse choice you can make for me.
Please help me.

   Sincerely,

     Your Alcoholic

Understanding Intervention

Intervention is a collective effort by the significant people
in an addict's life—family, friends, and co-workers—to
head off a crisis through respectful confrontation, sometimes referred to as "carefrontation." In its most basic
form, an intervention can be a meeting between a supervisor and an employee to candidly discuss problematic
behaviors or performance issues related to alcohol or
drug use. It also can be an orchestrated gathering of concerned co-workers or friends. Sometimes, an intervention
takes place during a performance review. There are many
ways to intervene on an employee in trouble. When infor-
mal methods don't work, or denial is operating in full
force, a formal intervention is necessary. That's the focus of
this book. This level of intervention is usually facilitated
by a professional interventionist and is designed to remove defensive obstructions to recovery. As part of the
process, participants address their possible mismanage-
ment of the disease or their own enabling behavior.

   A formal intervention can be the most effective way to
penetrate an employee's denial, which blocks the employee from seeking help on his or her own. Denial represents the single largest barrier to the diagnosis, referral,
and treatment of workplace addiction. While a significant

challenge for the addicted employee, it reaches far beyond the individual. For most of the twentieth century, American society denied that alcoholism was a problem. By not acknowledging its existence, families, communities, and employers avoided having to address it. Remnants of this denial mentality have carried over into the twenty-first century, fostering a mindset that's difficult to overcome.

When addiction invades a person's family, work group, or circle of friends, he or she often seeks the counsel of a trusted advisor. Sometimes that person is a clergy member, counselor, or family physician. The confidant can also be an EAP, boss, financial advisor, or attorney. It's important that these frontline people have a working knowledge of addiction, intervention, and treatment. They form the collective lifeline that tethers addicted employees and their families to the solid ground of recovery. It's also important that the public understand the role of intervention in addressing addiction. Prominent chemical dependency treatment centers around the country—including the Hazelden Foundation, the Betty Ford Center, and the Caron Foundation—advocate intervention as a means of jump-starting the recovery process. Intervention is effective because it overcomes the built-in denial factor that prevents impaired persons from understanding or accepting the reality of their illness. It removes defensive obstacles to recovery.

Roots of Intervention

Dr. Vernon Johnson, a Minneapolis minister who devoted his life to helping people overcome addictions, developed the first clinical process of intervention in the early 1960s. His concept was born out of compassion. He believed that it was both possible and essential to get alcoholics and addicts the clinical help they needed before they "hit rock bottom" and asked for it on their own. Hitting bottom means losing everything—family, job, home, and self-respect. While the bottom is different for every addict, it generally means that they have compromised themselves, destroyed relationships that were important to them, and headed for financial ruin.

Johnson's approach, originally called the Johnson Institute Model of Intervention, "raised the bottom" for thousands of alcoholics and addicts around the world—in every profession, across every industry, and at every level. Minimum-wage dishwashers, middle-aged cab drivers, aspiring CPAs, men and women of the cloth, elementary teachers, traveling sales managers, hair stylists, Washington bureaucrats, and company presidents—all have reclaimed their lives and careers after undergoing intervention, treatment, and recovery from addiction. The process works, regardless of gender, age, race, or occupation. It's no exaggeration to say that the intervention process revolutionized the field of chemical dependency treatment.

Johnson conceived of intervention as "a design for a cohesive group of friends and family to take a stand with the alcoholic, and present specific facts of his/her drinking in a loving and caring way, coupled with an offer for immediate help."[1] His design is chronicled in two landmark books, *Intervention: How to Help Someone Who Doesn't Want Help* (The Johnson Institute/Hazelden, 1989), and *I'll Quit Tomorrow* (HarperCollins, 1990). He also produced an excellent 90-minute intervention video that's currently being updated and adapted for the workplace. Clinicians still use Johnson's approach, and its many offshoots, to move alcoholics, addicts, and their families into the healing embrace of treatment.

Gauging Effectiveness

The first question that employers ask about intervention is how well it works. I polled members of the National Association of Independent Interventionists at the 1996 conference to get their opinion. The consensus was that 90 percent of professionally facilitated interventions resulted in direct admissions into treatment. This high admission rate is important, because treatment is the most direct path to recovery. The interventionists who participated in the poll employed a mix of intervention techniques, both in family settings and corporate. Their clients covered all ages, both sexes, and a wide range of economic and ethnic groups.[2] Their experiences match my own—which encompasses thousands of interventions in twenty countries and across most business sectors.

In chemical dependency circles, the professionally facilitated intervention process is recognized as one of the first steps to recovery. Among the public and employers, however, intervention is still a well-kept secret. One explanation is its relative newness. Though formally introduced in the 1960s, intervention is a latecomer in the clinical treatment process. Another reason relates to people's need to know. Until an individual comes face to face with the monster of addiction, he or she doesn't need information on how to slay it. Most are in the dark about the disease, its effects, and its impact on the workplace. Finally, corporate America is just beginning to recognize addiction as a significant business issue, one that drags down productivity, safety, and profitability. Until recently, the corporate world considered alcoholism and addiction a street, family, or medical issue. Each was clearly outside its purview. Growing awareness of the enormity and cost of workplace addiction is changing that view. With awareness comes understanding. Widespread adoption of intervention as a critical first step in treating workplace addiction is on the horizon.

Success in Treatment after Intervention

Success in the intervention process is one thing. Success in treatment is another. Results vary widely, depending on the individual, the severity of the addiction, and the circumstances of his or her work and personal life. Some afflicted employees go through multiple rounds of treatment before walking away from addiction for good. Others make the break after completing only one program. Still others never recover. Despite disparate track records, treatment programs—coupled with Twelve Step recovery programs—are still the best-known antidotes for addiction. And intervention is one of the most effective ways of moving employees toward recovery.

When employees enter treatment programs as a direct result of a professionally facilitated intervention, they are frequently referred to as "intervened employees." When employees seek treatment on their own, they are considered "self-referred." My research suggests that intervened employees have the same chance of benefiting from treatment as self-referred employees.[3] This finding contradicts the long-held belief that helping addicts before they ask for it is futile. In a study conducted in 1995, I compared the ability of two groups of in-patient men to perform normal tasks encountered in treatment. The first group consisted of ten self-referred employees from different companies and professions. The second was made up of ten intervened employees, also representing a variety of businesses and career tracks. The intervened group performed as well as the self-referred group in every area. The results were validated by independent interviews with on-site counselors.

There are six reasons that intervened employees perform on par with self-referred employees in treatment:

1. *Education.* The process of intervention does a better job of educating the intervention team about the disease of alcoholism or addiction. This enables team members to identify ways that they may have mismanaged the disease or enabled it to continue. Awareness enables everyone involved to make different choices and change behaviors.

2. *Healthy boundaries.* The intervention process sets very clear workplace boundaries and expectations. Managers and supervisors communicate in detail how things will change if the employee does not participate in the recovery process. This clarity can motivate the employee to work diligently on his or her program of recovery.

3. *Reality check.* The intervention process breaks through the employee's denial system. Like the Wizard of Oz, the false self that acts out destructive behaviors is revealed. The process of intervention serves as a reality check that exposes altered perceptions.

4. *Enlightenment.* Important clinical information surfaces in the intervention process. It helps the clinical team make an accurate assessment and design a successful treatment plan.

5. *Family healing.* Intervention marks the beginning of the family's recovery process. Its recovery takes root while the employee is in treatment.

6. *No second guessing.* Intervened employees are rarely "overdiagnosed" or "misdiagnosed." By the time a colleague, boss, friend, or family member calls in a professional interventionist, several other failed attempts to address the problem have been made. The problem is real.

Evolving Role of the Interventionist

In the early years of clinical interventions, intervention was a stand-alone event. Once the meeting concluded and the employee entered treatment or an AA program, there was no additional contact with the interventionist and little reference to the actual intervention during treatment. Intervention had no link to the primary treatment process. Today, most clinicians view the interventionist as an integral participant in the employee's continuum of care. The interventionist has access to important clinical information as a direct result of the intervention. The clinical team often references this information when preparing a comprehensive assessment and treatment plan after admission. The clinical team also relies on this information when outlining an aftercare program. Having been involved in the employee's life prior to treatment, the interventionist is aware of issues that could impact the employee's long-term recovery. For instance, an employee who returns to a company that just went through a merger might find that environment too unsettling. A cross-country trucker who lost his commercial license after being cited for driving while under the influence of alcohol will be unable to drive transport vehicles upon leaving treatment. Follow-up care will have to anticipate his need for retraining and the possible onset of depression triggered by the career loss. Interventionists also have insight into an employee's home life and support system. This has a major bearing on the employee's ability to stay on track.

In many cases, the interventionist acts as a liaison between the employee, treatment center, company, and family—providing that the employee has signed information release forms authorizing the treatment center to communicate with the interventionist. This liaison relationship, often referred to as "co-case management," adds another layer of accountability to the recovery process. Companies value it as a means of staying connected during treatment. It also helps supervisors better understand the recovery process and set reasonable expectations when the employee returns to work.

When the interventionist stays involved as a co-case manager, he or she must respect the boundaries set by the treatment team of the clinic or hospital. His or her role is that of liaison, not counselor. Wearing both hats could create conflict among the team and confusion for the employee. With clear understanding of who does what, the team can work together without overstepping responsibilities.

The Intervention Process

Although there are several models of intervention being practiced today, most include the five basic steps listed below. A more detailed discussion follows the list.

1. *Selecting the interventionist.* The first step is to identify the right professional to facilitate the process. It's best to bring in someone from the outside who has no ties to the organization and can be objective.

2. *Planning the intervention.* The interventionist begins by helping the company's point person select team members. Having a large group is less important than having the right people. Other tasks include choosing the dates of the intervention, coordinating with the team members and treatment provider, making necessary travel plans, confirming insurance coverage, and making financial arrangements.

3. *Pre-intervention meeting.* This meeting involves the intervention team but not the impaired employee. Its purpose is to educate and prepare the participants for

the upcoming intervention. Good planning and preparation are a must.

4. *The intervention.* This is when the team members and interventionist meet with the alcoholic or addict. They present information in a respectful manner, withholding judgments. All information relates to the employee's work performance and behaviors. It is important not to blame, shame, or deliberately make the employee feel worse about the situation. The idea is not to punish the employee but to enable him or her to receive help in overcoming the disease.

5. *Admission into treatment.* If insurance coverage is not in question and preadmission work is done in advance, the interventionist accompanies the intervened employee directly to the treatment center. More often, the company's managed care provider or insurance carrier requires a separate chemical dependency assessment before referring the employee to a treatment program. This can slow down the process by several weeks.

SELECTING THE INTERVENTIONIST

The field of intervention has its share of rogues. To guard against self-proclaimed interventionists with dubious credentials, avoid Lone Rangers who operate outside the bounds of professional circles. The marks of a true professional are a willingness to have work reviewed by a panel of peers, a commitment to professional development, and the active involvement of an outside coach or supervisor.

For starters, the interventionist must be educated, skilled, and experienced in planning and facilitating interventions for businesses and organizations. The intervention process is both sensitive and critical, so it's no time to call in favors from a well-meaning friend or colleague who's good at facilitating. Nor is this the time to use an insider, no matter how knowledgeable the person might be about addiction. A professional interventionist from outside the organization will bring a completely objective perspective to the process. This helps when people with different personalities are involved and emotions are highly charged. The interventionist brings a wealth of experience from past interventions to the table. This experience can be extremely useful in strategizing an approach, since most participants have little or no prior experience in running interventions.

To be effective, the interventionist can't just rush in and confront someone about his or her substance abuse problem. That would do more harm than good. He or she must find out as much about the employee's work and personal situation as possible—usually in as little time as possible. An unsettling incident or crisis usually precipitates the need for an intervention, so lead time is a luxury.

The following checklist is provided to help managers evaluate prospective interventionists and choose the person best suited to guide the process.

Interventionist Checklist

Education
- ❑ Advanced degree(s)
- ❑ Specialized training areas
- ❑ Supervised clinical counseling experience in area of specialty

Certification
- ❑ License or certification in chemical dependency counseling or treating addictions
- ❑ Reputable certifying organization
- ❑ Professional affiliations or memberships

Experience
- ❏ Scope of experience in providing intervention services
- ❏ Years of experience in providing intervention services
- ❏ Number of interventions facilitated

Fee Structure
- ❏ Cost for facilitating an intervention
- ❏ Means of payment—check, cash, insurance reimbursement, and so on
- ❏ Terms of payment—prepayment, payment on demand, installments, and so on

Approach
- ❏ Model of intervention used
- ❏ Steps in the process
- ❏ Primary populations served—corporate clients, teens, women, and so on

Ongoing Involvement
- ❏ Length of involvement after the intervention
- ❏ Preplanning and aftercare services

Professional References
- ❏ Reputable treatment centers
- ❏ Past clients
- ❏ Professional associations

Insurance
- ❏ Malpractice insurance

PLANNING THE INTERVENTION

Much of the critical work of the intervention is done prior to the face-to-face meeting with the impaired employee. The interventionist begins with a battery of tactical questions. The answers help construct the framework for a successful intervention. Participants can expect to field the following questions:

- Where will the planning meeting and the intervention be staged?
- Who are the most appropriate people to participate in the intervention process and form the intervention team?
- Which health care provider is best suited to provide clinical services to treat the impaired employee?
- Where does the employee's insurance carrier recommend that treatment be provided? Will it cover residential or outpatient programs? What about aftercare?
- Will the managed care provider require an independent chemical dependency assessment prior to making a treatment referral?
- How aware of the problem is the employee's family? Should any family members be included in the intervention process?
- What are the consequences if the employee refuses treatment?
- What specific evidence of the employee's substance abuse problem has been documented—especially related to measurable job performance?
- Is this the first time the employee has been treated for a chemical addiction?
- Are there medical or psychological concerns that might affect the intervention approach or outcome?
- Is there any risk of violence?
- How will the treatment be paid for (insurance, private pay)?
- What specific requirements must the employee meet in order to resume his or her job with the company?

Team members need to be very specific about why the company is intervening on the employee. They may site absenteeism, evidence of intoxication, deterioration in work standards, complaints from customers or other employees, or incidents of insubordination. Specific examples make it harder for the employee to dodge the issue with vague excuses or turn the blame on another employee. I encourage team members to write out their observations prior to the actual intervention. The exercise of writing things down helps them organize their thoughts, so they can present them in a manner that is compelling and well received. It also ensures that important issues don't get overlooked. Written notes provide a crutch for getting through sensitive information that is hard to deliver. They also enable team members to edit out statements that are judgmental, harsh, or accusatory. A professionally facilitated intervention is a clinical process, not a trial. It's designed to identify the problem and deliver help, not punish the offender.

Two vital pieces of information emerge from this fact-finding mission. The first relates to consequences. If the employee refuses help after it has been offered, what's the next step? It's wise to involve legal counsel in reviewing the options, which are limited. They can include probation, a leave of absence, and termination. The second involves action. If the employee agrees to receive help, he or she enters a treatment and recovery program. Some addicts attempt to bargain their way out of treatment by promising to give up the chemical. Abstinence only addresses one symptom of the disease, the drug or alcohol. A treatment program is necessary to change errant behaviors and heal all the related symptoms of the addiction.

While co-workers or supervisors most often initiate workplace interventions, family members can prompt the same action. They sometimes recognize signs of addiction at home long before they manifest themselves at work. They may contact someone at work to validate their concerns and ask for help—especially after they have tried and failed numerous times to address the problem on their own. They believe, with good reason, that the addict's employer will carry more sway because the employer controls the purse strings. When family members play the role of initiator, they almost always serve on the intervention team.

THE PRE-INTERVENTION MEETING

Once the team establishes the five Ws of intervention— who, what, when, where, and why—it can concentrate on how. This is the strategic phase of the planning process. Everyone on the intervention team attends the strategy meeting. The interventionist facilitates, explaining what's expected of each participant and why.

The first part of this meeting is educational. It starts with an overview of the "disease concept" of alcohol or drug addiction—including symptoms, progression of the disease, enabling behavior, codependency, the dry drunk syndrome, and organizational dynamics. This gives everyone on the team a shared knowledge base and limits the chances of members being at cross-purposes. The interventionist augments the disease discussion with a brief introduction to the intervention process. He or she may also describe the particular treatment center where the employee will be admitted, if this is known in advance. Having a sense of how long the employee will be in treatment, how the program works, and when they can call or visit puts team members more at ease. This education session is most productive when it's interactive. Participants are encouraged to ask questions and give feedback.

During the second half of the meeting, the team prepares for the intervention itself. To be successful, the intervention needs to be well planned and carefully cast. Every team member has an assigned part and a moment in the spotlight. Each needs to be clear on who says what so the intervention doesn't turn into a free-for-all. An intervention is more like a well-rehearsed one-act than improvisational theater. Nine concerns listed below will be discussed in the pre-intervention meeting:

- Introduction of participants
- Goal of the intervention process
- Summary of the disease concept
- Affects of alcoholism and addiction on work and personal life
- Information sharing on the impaired employee
- Plan for the intervention meeting
- Written assignments to prepare for the intervention
- Overview of the treatment process
- Discussion of aftercare options

THE INTERVENTION

This is the heart of the intervention process. It represents the first time the intervention team meets face-to-face with the impaired employee. The primary objective is to get the employee into treatment. The secondary objective is to clearly communicate the company's boundaries so the employee understands what's at stake.

The interventionist facilitates the meeting, prompting each person on when to speak and responding to the intervened employee. He or she keeps the intervention on track and prevents the process from taking on a negative tone. Team members share only what they have rehearsed during the pre-intervention meeting. The information should pertain directly to the impaired employee's work performance. General observations that cannot be substantiated are counterproductive. Information about the employee's personal life is mostly irrelevant, unless the family is involved in the intervention. Team members should resist the temptation to speculate on things the employee might have done, or things that could have happened as a result of drinking. Conjecture is taboo. For the process to work, the employee needs to understand that the observations are based on fact. Everyone should be familiar with the process and know what to expect (see agenda below).

- Company representative introduces interventionist
- Interventionist explains the intervention process to impaired employee
- Interventionist presents potential treatment plan
- Team members present prepared notes
- Interventionist explains potential consequences to impaired employee
- Initiated by interventionist, impaired employee decides to participate in or decline recovery plan
- Interventionist concludes the intervention
- Admission into a treatment program, coordinated by interventionist, or initiation of an independent chemical dependency assessment

ADMISSION INTO TREATMENT

If the intervention goes as expected, and insurance issues don't slow down the process, the intervened employee enters treatment immediately after the meeting ends. This can be done as an inpatient or outpatient, meaning the employee stays overnight or spends only day hours in treatment. Treatment can last a few weeks or several months, depending on the employee.

In today's managed care environment, most intervened employees must undergo a separate assessment before being referred to a treatment program. This assessment, while valuable, can delay the start of treatment by several weeks. During this time, the employee often continues to use and can take out his or her resentments on co-workers, family members, or himself or herself. The delay puts people at risk. Whenever possible, it's advisable to get the employee into treatment immediately following the intervention.

Not every intervention is successful. Sometimes the denial factor is so strong, or the fear of being discovered so overpowering, that the employee chooses the negative consequences over going through treatment. In many cases, this means walking away from his or her job.

The Bottom Line

Janet was chief financial officer for a large East Coast paper manufacturer for twelve years. She survived two recessions, one union strike, and the most profitable stretch in the company's history. Her responsibilities changed when it launched an ambitious growth-through-acquisition strategy in early 1999. She devoted many evenings to reviewing the balance sheets of small paper companies that might be ripe for a takeover. She also was required to give regular financial presentations at the early morning management meetings.

While Janet enjoyed her more visible role, she found that the increased demands cramped her style. She no longer felt free to duck out early for happy hour at her favorite pub, or slip in late when she'd tipped too many the night before. She started stashing a flask in her desk drawer, in case she couldn't get away or the pressures of corporate raiding got too much for her. She had another in her glove compartment, and a third in her briefcase for the train ride home.

In August, the company completed its first acquisition. The executive team went out to celebrate while the ink dried on the agreement. The next morning, one of Janet's colleagues pulled her aside to express his concern about her drinking. It'd gotten excessive, he said, and was spilling into the office. He hinted that he wasn't alone in his concern. She laughed it off, assuring him that she could handle her liquor as well as any member of the executive team. She acknowledged that she probably indulged a bit too heartily from time to time, but passed it off as a pressure reliever.

Over the next six months, the company bought two more paper plants and Janet was buried in paperwork and filing deadlines. As the pressure grew, so did her drinking. She attempted to be discreet, ducking into the lady's room when she needed a quick swig. She assured herself that no one noticed. She drank a little every day, just to get through. A little turned into a lot. She began to lose her edge, missing critical deadlines, and making sloppy financial errors. In one week, she botched the projections on a major expansion opportunity, slept through the company's annual meeting, and was fined by the IRS for significantly underpaying quarterly income taxes. When the loan officer from the company's primary lending institution called the president to complain about Janet's lack of professionalism and frequent outbursts, the company felt compelled to intervene.

The president called an experienced interventionist to guide the process. Together, they identified the intervention team—three members of the management team, the human resources director, the lead accountant from Janet's department, the company's corporate counsel, and the president. Janet didn't have much contact with her family, so they weren't included. No one on the management team knew enough about her private life to risk involving friends.

In preparation for the intervention, the team drafted a list of ten specific, documented incidents of work-related drinking. Members decided in advance who would say what and how to couch the message so that it made a strong impression but wasn't shaming. When first confronted with the team's concerns, Janet denied that she had any difficulty with alcohol. The intervention team had anticipated a swift denial and presented her with written evidence that its members had gathered in advance. After listening to the list, Janet was speechless. With great difficulty, she admitted that the team was probably right. Her drinking problem had adversely affected her work performance. Once she got beyond her own denial system, she saw the bottom line—a daily dependence on alcohol, an inability to manage the responsibilities of her job, unreliable performance, unpredictable emotional outbursts, and more. She understood that she needed help.

Within six hours of the crisis intervention, Janet was admitted to the women's program at a reputable treatment center for chemical dependency rehabilitation. She agreed to complete a one-month program as a condition of her return to work. The company agreed to keep her job open. It valued her skills and experience and wanted to see her become a productive member of the management team again. The timely, well-orchestrated intervention made that possible. After Janet completed treatment, she returned to her job with a renewed spirit and an attitude of gratitude.

4

Models of Intervention

In the last thirty years, professionals in the chemical dependency field have refined the original Johnson Institute model of intervention to match the needs of different individuals and situations. Every intervention is unique. No single approach works for all people. What's appropriate in a family setting may be ill suited for a corporate environment. What's comfortable for some cultural groups would be out of order for others. Even the gender of the interventionist can make a difference. In the case of the female employee who has a history of drug addiction and physical abuse, a female interventionist might be better received than a male. Any variation on the intervention theme that respects the employee and ensures a more favorable outcome is viable.

The intervention team has only one chance to stage an effective intervention. If the meeting gets botched because the method didn't match the circumstances, or the team wasn't adequately prepared, the opportunity is lost. The team can't come back two weeks later for a retake. This show is live. The need to do it right the first time makes a strong argument for using a professional interventionist. He or she has the experience to guide the intervening company on which model to use, who to invite, and how to finesse the details to achieve optimal results. Untrained interventionists can only guess and hope for the best. Employees' lives and companies' futures are at stake. There is no room for trial and error.

Professionally facilitated interventions have an unusually high success rate of getting employees into treatment. Some research puts it as high as 90 percent. A 1999 study by the University of New Mexico[1] tempers this statistic, suggesting that other family-initiated intervention techniques are more effective, at least in family settings. The topic of how best to arrest the disease continues to be the subject of academic research and clinical debate. In cases where the intervened employee refuses treatment, the company ends up enforcing the boundaries established prior to the intervention. This generally means termination. Either way, the company comes out ahead because it has proactively dealt with an issue that has put the organization, the afflicted employee, and numerous stakeholders at risk.

While family interventions have been happening for decades, corporate interventions are a relatively recent phenomenon. Only in the last few years have organizations discovered the power of the intervention process to make employees productive again. Most corporate interventions follow one of three approaches: the carefrontation model, the invitational model, and the executive model. While there are commonalities among all three, each differs in substance, format, and style.

The Carefrontation Model of Intervention

Carefrontation is a popular variation on the original Johnson Institute model of intervention. This "caring approach to confrontation" emphasizes the same respectful, non-shaming core values that Johnson espoused, but has benefited from thirty years of refinement. One improvement is that carefrontation encourages team members to frame all observations about the intervened employee from the "I" perspective. The traditional "you" approach can come off as accusatory and judgmental. Consider the following I-based statement: "I have seen your ability to communicate with your co-workers deteriorate as a result of your alcoholism." This is much easier for the intervened employee to accept than its you-based alternative: "You don't know how to communicate anymore." The former is factual and nonemotional, the latter blame-laden. Using "I" versus "you" language makes the intervention team's message infinitely more palatable. It enables the employee to hear what's been said without getting defensive, and neutralizes the need to erect emotional brick walls. Emotional barriers cause interference. They distract from the aim of getting the employee to recognize his or her addiction and accept the offer of help.

Carefrontation is the most widely used model of intervention in the American workplace. It works in a variety of applications and at most levels of a company. Carefrontation follows the basic format outlined in chapter 3. It starts by retaining an interventionist and coordinating the details of the intervention—including the assembly of the intervention team. The next step focuses on educating the team and mapping out a strategy for the actual intervention. At the end of this two- or three-hour session, each member knows what to say and when to speak. The last steps are the intervention itself and admission into treatment.

The distinguishing feature of the carefrontation model is that the addicted employee is *not* told about the intervention in advance. He or she doesn't learn about it until arriving at the meeting. The interventionist, acting as facilitator, opens by stating the reason for the gathering—to address the employee's substance abuse problem. He or she manages the information flow and responds to the employee's cross talk and denial. The interventionist coaches members of the intervention team to stick to the information they prepared in advance. This minimizes the risk of participants engaging in verbal jousting which, like emotional walls, distracts from the meeting's focus and can sabotage the process. An effective interventionist needs sound judgment, firmness of purpose, and a compassionate heart to bring the intervention to a successful conclusion.

The average carefrontation intervention lasts an hour or less. While each is unique, all end by offering the intervened employee an immediate plan for recovery. This decision is not left up to the employees themselves. Because of the illness, they are incapable of masterminding their own recovery.

The Invitational Model of Intervention

The invitational model of corporate intervention emerged in the last few years as a no-surprise alternative to the traditional carefrontation approach. It differs in that the company tells the impaired employee in advance of its intention to do an intervention. The verbal invitation to attend states that the company recognizes the existence of a substance abuse problem and feels compelled to address it. The spokesperson makes it clear that the company will take action *whether or not* the employee chooses to participate. Given the firm tone of the invitation, the addicted employee rarely declines to attend. In contrast, addicted family members who are invited to their own intervention may refuse to take part. That's because the family has less leverage than an employer does to oblige attendance. Family interventions need to draw upon a different set of motivating factors, including continuation of the marriage, financial support, or relationship.

Preparation is the trademark of any successful invitational intervention. It's not uncommon for the team to hold several planning sessions in advance of the actual intervention. At least one takes place before the invitation is extended. Unlike carefrontations, invitational interventions focus less on the addict or alcoholic and more on the organization where the impaired employee works. Addiction afflicts more than just the user. The entire system needs to be healed.

The primary advantage of the invitational model is that it alleviates the need to surprise the addicted employee. Staff members don't have to create a pretense to get the employee to attend the meeting. Nor must they hold hushed planning sessions in the days or weeks preceding the intervention. Everything is out in the open. The employee is informed of the consequences from the outset and makes choices accordingly. If he or she chooses not to participate in the intervention process, the consequences remain in force. They could be anything from a written warning, to probation, to immediate termination. The fact that the company has formally addressed the employee's alcoholism or addiction provides some protection if the employee later resists the consequences or attempts legal reprisal against the employer. A detailed discussion of legal issues related to workplace addiction follows in chapter 6.

Invitation for Recovery

Lee was a litigator in a sixty-person law firm that specialized in health care and employment law. He had a history of alcohol-related problems as long as his client list, and everyone in the organization knew it. With the exception of his drinking, Lee was considered a valuable member of the practice. He had a knack for bringing in new clients. He knew his way around the law library as well as the courtroom. He'd joined the firm right out of law school, when the practice had a few hospital clients and was based in the emerging warehouse district. Lee helped build the firm into a respected practice in the core of downtown.

Despite Lee's numerous close calls with clients, none of the managing partners had been willing to confront him about his drinking. The associates didn't dare. Denial was at work. All that changed when a new client lodged a complaint with the state bar association about Lee's behavior during a recent consultation. The client, a large health maintenance organization (HMO) that the firm had been courting for years, reported that Lee smelled of alcohol, could not seem to track what was going on in the meeting, and responded to questions with noticeably slurred speech. It was 11 A.M. and he was drunk.

The potential fallout from this situation was enormous. The firm was in jeopardy of losing the client and having its reputation in health care tarnished. It also faced possible legal action due to Lee's incompetence while practicing law under the influence of alcohol. The partners were forced to take action.

After some late-night preparations with a professional interventionist, the partners invited Lee to attend a meeting scheduled for the express purpose of addressing his drinking problem. There they discussed the client complaint and presented other evidence of abuse, dating back at least five years. The interventionist facilitated the meeting, keeping the discussion focused and respectful. Lee insisted that the HMO incident had been a fluke and that he did not have an alcohol problem. He assured his colleagues that he could control his drinking and offered to draft a formal apology to the client and the bar association. He was in complete denial, unable to recognize the patterns of his addiction or the severity of his problem.

The meeting closed with the partners making Lee's employment contingent upon his immediate and successful completion of a treatment program and his ongoing participation in a recognized recovery program. Faced with no alternative, Lee reluctantly agreed. The partners and the interventionist regrouped after the meeting, drained but relieved. They had finally dealt with one of the most difficult decisions in their professional lives—how and when to confront a respected peer about his drinking problem. The action, while long overdue, was necessary to protect Lee, the firm, its clients, and its staff members.

At the firm's request, the interventionist stayed involved with Lee throughout treatment and into recovery. He kept the partners abreast of Lee's progress and mentored them on how to handle his reentry. As a result of the experience, the firm expanded its health care practice to include a chemical treatment facility and an urban shelter for people with drug and alcohol addictions. The latter was a pro bono client.

The Executive Model of Intervention

Interventionists employ the executive model when substance abuse hits a senior executive, up to and including the president and chief executive officer (CEO). This approach, more than either the carefrontation or invitational models, takes into account the scope of the executive's job responsibilities and the financial implications of unseating him or her, even temporarily. Much is at stake for both the executive and the company, so the intervention needs to go flawlessly. A misstep could spell disaster. In all circumstances, executive interventions should be facilitated by an experienced interventionist who is at ease in both the boardroom and executive suite.

Protective layers can make addicted executives difficult to reach. Rank, power, money, or stature often insulate them from the natural and logical consequences of their illness. These trappings can disguise symptoms and productivity issues, prolonging the period that addiction goes untreated. The disease can escalate to advanced stages before the company or family knows enough to intervene. Unlike employees in subordinate positions, executives have the option to delegate responsibilities when their addiction makes it impossible for them to perform. They can cancel projects and reprioritize others as a means of relieving pressure. They can ask their personal assistants to reschedule meetings, hold calls, or run interference when the realities of the addiction hinder their work. Unreasonable behavior either is tolerated because no one dares challenge the boss, or excused as a normal response to the pressures of the position. These buffers make it exceedingly difficult to identify the illness, let alone collect specific information to use in the intervention process. The higher the tree limb, the more easily the executive can camouflage the colors of his or her addiction in the protective foliage.

Executive interventions are complex. The interventionist must consider a number of sensitive issues in the planning process.

- *Team selection.* The makeup of the intervention team is crucial. It must include individuals who command the respect of the executive. If the intervened executive is someone other than the CEO, that person's supervisor or superior must be present. Otherwise, the executive may not take the intervention seriously or be moved to make a healthy decision regarding treatment. It is not unusual for board members, or a single representative from the board, to serve on the team. Their presence is essential, for they are the only people who outrank the

CEO and have the power to remove him or her from office. They carry the leverage needed to break the cycle of addiction. In rare cases, it may be best to restrict the intervention team to one or two people—assuming those individuals have the ear of the executive—to avoid creating panic in the executive ranks.

- *Shareholder interest.* For large corporations with publicly traded securities, the board of directors has a responsibility to safeguard the shareholders' interests. Decisions about how to handle the executive intervention must involve input from the board, corporate counsel, and the interventionist. The strategy should consider fiduciary responsibilities such as ensuring strong earnings or preserving potential merger opportunities.

- *Communication.* Working in tandem with the company's corporate communications staff or outside public relations firm, the intervention team should map out a plan for communicating the issue to internal and, if necessary, external constituents. Internal audiences include employees, board members, shareholders, financial and strategic partners, and key advisors such as accountants, bankers, and attorneys. External constituents may include customers, suppliers and vendors, industry associations, and the media.

If time allows, carefully worded news releases, e-mail announcements, and letters should be drafted in advance and distributed as soon as the intervention is complete. Time is of the essence. If word of the intervention hits the streets before the company has an opportunity to announce it, the organization is backed into a defensive mode. Its attention gets diverted from managing information to putting out fires.

It's important that communication respects the dignity

and privacy of the intervened executive while keeping people informed whose jobs, investments, and business relationships may be materially affected by the outcome of the intervention. Sometimes, news of the intervention is kept strictly confidential, except for those directly involved in the process. This is easier to accomplish if the intervened executive carries a low public profile or is not the CEO. Other times, the circumstances surrounding the intervention force the company to deal with it publicly. This was clearly the case when the publisher of a daily newspaper was arrested after a hit-and-run accident involving an excessively high blood alcohol level. The story made the news wires even before the police officer filed the accident report. The publisher's problem with alcohol was no longer a private issue. It was played out in the regional media. Communication at this stage was crisis management at best, damage control at worst. Another example involved the chief negotiator of a major West Coast plastics company who lost his temper during union negotiations and physically threatened the union's negotiator. The executive had a history of alcohol-related outbursts at work and an assault on his record. The incident made the national news, and the company was bombarded with calls from media, employees, and outraged union members from around the country. It had to respond.

- *Treatment providers.* In choosing the treatment provider for an intervened executive, it's helpful to find a center or program that has other executive-level participants. Their presence acts as both a mirror on reality and a source of peer-to-peer support for the intervened executive. Peers counter the delusion that the executive, by virtue of rank or title, is exempt from the rules of addiction. The principle of peer-to-peer treatment is based on the clinical process of "mirroring." It plays on the power of individuals to recognize their addiction by seeing it acted out in others—especially those whose backgrounds, ages, and positions resemble their own. This principle also applies to aftercare, which is covered in chapter 5. Simply put, employees have a much better chance of recovery if they can be treated around people like themselves.

- *Confidentiality and containment.* The highest level of confidentiality must be respected throughout the executive intervention process to protect both the executive and the company. The need for confidentiality is intensified because the executive tends to be in the public limelight. His or her actions readily attract the attention of the media and company watchdogs. This creates the potential for backlash that could be damaging to the company, either in dollars or reputation. The containment requirement applies to any behavior that is considered circumspect and all information that arises in the intervention process. Even if the information is not pertinent to the intervention, it must be held in confidence because of its potential to be misinterpreted or taken out of context. It's the responsibility of the interventionist to be judicious in probing for information and to instruct the intervention team on the need for absolute discretion. In deciding which information to reveal during the intervention, the litmus test is whether the information will move the intervened executive closer to getting the necessary help. Is it necessary or relevant?

- *Continued involvement.* Companies are strongly encouraged to keep the interventionist involved with the impaired executive as a co-case manager after the intervention. This liaison role adds accountability throughout the treatment process, which improves the likelihood of success. Some corporations even retain the

interventionist for up to a year after the executive fin-
ishes primary treatment to ensure that the aftercare
program is effective.

When intervening on executives, it's important to remember that the disease of alcoholism or drug addiction
is progressive and potentially fatal. Regardless of the executive's power, position, or past accomplishments, he or
she can die from untreated addiction as easily as a delivery clerk or any other member of a staff. Addiction is an
equal opportunity illness. The decision to take action is
heart wrenching, but saves lives and improves the health
of the entire workplace.

DWI Intervention

Larry is the joint venture project manager for an international electronics corporation headquartered in Atlanta. He
negotiates multimillion dollar contracts with suppliers and
manufacturing partners around the world. His colleagues
became concerned when Larry was picked up for driving
while under the influence. He was on his way home from a
three-day business trip to Brussels and had been downing
two-ounce bottles of scotch throughout the transatlantic
flight. Larry was embarrassed about the DWI, but passed
off his impaired driving as the result of jet lag. This was not
the first time that Larry had minimized his drinking. His
best friend, the company's product development manager,
had tried to talk to him about it several times over the last
few years. The words fell on deaf ears. So did the expres-
sions of concern by other managers in his department, especially those who traveled with him. No one could broach
the subject without raising Larry's defenses.

To his close associates, Larry appeared to be aging before their eyes. A natural athlete who had run in several

marathons, he had stopped running altogether. He had gained weight and always seemed to be battling some ailment or other. He began taking unexplained time off from work and missed several critical meetings. This slack attitude toward work was decidedly out of character for a classic Type A personality.

When his longtime administrative assistant noticed an empty bottle of scotch in his desk drawer, she called the human resources director to seek advice. She was ambivalent, torn between her sense of loyalty to Larry and her distress over his deteriorating health. The HR director called the division head, to whom Larry reported. The news was disturbing but not surprising, the latest in a series of alcohol-related problems that marred an otherwise stellar record. Larry's boss decided it was time to act. He called in a respected corporate interventionist who recently had rescued the head of a nonprofit board on which he served.

The division head didn't want to initiate any action that might affect a valued member of the business development team—and the future of the company's international contracts—without the support of the board of directors. Having never been through an intervention at this level, the board relied on the interventionist for guidance. At her urging, it invited two members of the executive staff to serve on the intervention team. They had firsthand knowledge of Larry's drinking habits and eroding work performance. The team briefly discussed the possibility of inviting Larry's wife to participate, but decided against it. She tended to drink heavily at company functions, and they didn't want her to sabotage the intervention to protect her husband.

Everyone pledged to keep the matter in the strictest confidence. Each team member documented evidence that would help convince Larry that he needed help. The board authorized use of the corporate plane to deliver Larry to a treatment center in Florida after the intervention.

When Larry walked into the meeting, his antennae went up. He knew from the unusual mix of men and women seated around the conference table that something unexpected was on the agenda. The interventionist introduced herself and explained that the group had gathered out of concern for Larry and his drinking. Sticking to the plan, each member took turns sharing carefully prepared statements. Then the interventionist presented the plan for Larry's treatment and recovery. Without hesitation, Larry agreed, surprising a few members of the team who were primed for objections.

Prior to flying out, Larry called his wife to tell her what was happening. He and the interventionist stopped by his house a half hour later to share the details of the recovery plan. It included Larry's primary treatment and an intensive family treatment program for his wife. Seeing that Larry had signed off on the plan, she breathed a sigh of relief and cosigned the plan.

The Importance of Consequences

Every model of intervention calls for setting clear boundaries or consequences. Boundaries let the person being intervened on know exactly what will happen if he or she refuses the offer of help. They also put all the team members on the same page. The need for concrete boundaries is born out of the disease of alcoholism and addiction itself. It is said to breed in vagueness, secrecy, and darkness. The more specific the consequences, the better for everyone involved. In many instances, it's smart to present the consequences in writing. Both the employee and a company representative sign the document, agreeing to the terms discussed. This avoids confusion and heads off eleventh-hour efforts to renegotiate the deal after the intervention is over. A written, signed agreement also provides a measure of legal protection for the employer. In setting and enforcing boundaries with intervened employees, the organization sends a clear message that it will not enable an employee's illness. This stance represents a healthy value system that confronts and counters dysfunction.

Intervening in Absentia

When assembling an intervention team on short notice, it's sometimes difficult to get everyone together in one room at the same time. Travel plans, illness, distance, or business responsibilities make attendance impractical. People who are physically unavailable can still participate by drafting a letter to the intervened employee and having it read in absentia at the intervention meeting. Technology also allows absent team members to participate over a speakerphone or by videoconference. While not as immediate as personal attendance, these options are viable alternatives for businesses equipped with the necessary communications equipment.

Letters should express two main emotions—concern and support. After acknowledging the existence of the employee's substance abuse problem and citing evidence, the authors should encourage the employee to accept help. Letters follow the same format as notes written by team members who attend the actual intervention.

Common Objections

Most interventions will encounter some degree of resistance from the employee being intervened on. Sometimes this resistance is based on a case of "terminal uniqueness." People with this attitude believe they are truly different than everyone else on the planet. They think that they are endowed with a special ability to handle their alcohol or drug addiction problem on their own. Their logic goes something like this: "I see what works for you other guys, but my case is different. Don't you know who I am? I'm special." This mindset can be a deadly deterrent to recovery because it prevents the addicted employee from recognizing and surrendering to the disease.

Other common responses encountered during intervention include the following:

- I'm too busy to take time off for treatment.
- My drinking isn't that bad. I know other people who are in worse shape than me.
- My problem is not affecting anyone but me.
- Alcoholics and drug addicts are on skid row. I hold down a respectable job and support my family. I am not an alcoholic.
- I only use alcohol, not drugs, so the problem can't be that bad.
- I only use chemicals on the weekend.
- I have to drink to do my job effectively. I entertain clients.
- I'll quit on my own.
- I have only done cocaine once.
- I'll quit using drugs and just drink alcohol.
- What will people think if I go away for treatment?
- I'll be fired if I admit my problem and get treatment.
- I'll go into treatment next month.
- My chemical dependency problems will be gone when my divorce is final, my kids move out, or my boss retires.

It's normal for the impaired employee to attempt to throw the intervention off track by getting into a verbal sparring match with team members. Some members are emotionally charged and can lose objectivity if they get drawn into disruptive conversation. It's best for the professional interventionist to handle any objections that come up during the intervention. He or she has heard every excuse imaginable and is adept at fielding them.

Employee Assistance Professionals

For an employee whose life has become unmanageable because of drugs or alcohol, or a manager trying to deal with the fallout of that employee's addiction, knowing where to turn for advice is of great value. One of the first stops is the company's employee assistance program (EAP). Run by trained employee assistance professionals, this program is designed to help managers identify and resolve a wide range of workplace problems related to productivity, performance, and misconduct. The source of the problems may be health, marriage, family, finances, alcohol, drugs, legal difficulties, emotional issues, stress, or other personal concerns. EAPs also assist employees' family members. They play a major role in addressing employee drug or alcohol problems in the workplace. EAP professionals often are asked to identify a suitable interventionist or treatment provider for the afflicted employee. Occasionally, they serve on the intervention team, although it's more typical for them to work on the sidelines. This distance enables them to play a supportive role after the employee completes treatment.

More than 85 percent of Fortune 500 companies have EAPs in-house. Smaller companies contract with independent EAP providers for this service. Companies do so as a benefit to their employees and a way of ensuring that their workforce operates at peak performance. EAPs save companies money through lower rates on accidents, health plan use, and workers' compensation costs. The annual cost per employee is under $27 for an in-house EAP, under $22 for an outside EAP.[2] Compared to the cost of recruiting, hiring, and training a new employee, estimated at $50,000 per year, these costs are minimal.[3] The National Clearinghouse for Alcohol and Drug Information (NCADI) estimates that for every $1 the employer invests in an EAP, the company saves between $5 and $16.[4]

Outside Counsel

On a snowy day in early December, a group of business-people gathered in the suburban Chicago offices of an independent EAP professional for an introductory meeting. The group, made up of investors and management staff members of a small software development company, was preparing to intervene on the firm's chief software designer. Marlene was a whiz kid with uncanny programming skills and a serious drinking problem. The staff had addressed her drinking on several occasions and took heart in the apparent improvements she had made. Unfortunately, the core problem never went away. It got progressively worse as the business grew and pressure to perform mounted. Marlene's addiction threatened to stall the next major software release, a death knell for time-sensitive technology products that compete on Internet time.

The board had decided to do an intervention as a final attempt to correct the problem and salvage the launch. The firm was too small to support its own human resource department or EAP, so it contracted with an independent employee assistance professional named Joan.

As an outsider, Joan could offer candid advice about

the intervention process without worrying about breaking allegiances. Her objectivity helped board members see beyond their personal and professional relationships with Marlene to do what was right for the company and her. After listening to their observations and concerns, Joan recommended the names of two interventionists for them to consider. She also suggested a well-known clinic that offered both inpatient and outpatient treatment options. Most important, she offered support, consultation, and education on the disease of alcoholism and the opportunities for treatment. Not all of the board members were knowledgeable about the disease. Some questioned the wisdom of intervening on Marlene before she bottomed out. Others had unrealistic expectations, thinking that a few weeks in treatment would cure her. Joan walked the middle ground, encouraging them to intervene on Marlene early to arrest the disease, while reminding them that addiction was treatable but not curable. She was an informed voice of reason in the midst of confusion.

The board was not alone in its inexperience with addiction and intervention. Regardless of job level or education, most businesspeople are naïve on the subject. This void in their experience breeds anxiety and uncertainty. Joan was able to calm their concern and unite their efforts.

Corporate counsel had drawn up a last-chance contract in preparation for Marlene's intervention. Seeing that her only option was to walk away from the product that she had created, Marlene agreed to the terms. Before she could enter treatment, she had to undergo an independent chemical dependency assessment mandated by the firm's managed care provider. It confirmed the prognosis and referred her to a five-week inpatient program. Then she transitioned into a structured aftercare program that included individual counseling and active participation in Alcoholics Anonymous. She stuck with it, knowing that her position with the company was contingent upon her continued abstinence and recovery.

One of the most important services that EAPs provide is training for managers and supervisors. They coach decision makers on how to run prevention programs, wellness and balance programs, crisis assessments, and referrals. EAPs also serve as valued resources to managers, executives, supervisors, and unions who need guidance. The existence of EAPs sends a positive message to employees that the company is interested in their well-being and committed to helping them cope with personal issues and crises that may affect their job. This support mechanism makes employees feel more secure and valued, so they stay longer and do better work.

EAP Services

- Expert consultation and training in the identification and resolution of a wide range of job performance issues
- Confidential, appropriate, and timely assessment services
- Referrals for appropriate diagnosis, treatment, and assistance
- Links between the workplace and community resources
- Follow-up services for employees who use treatment services
- Coordination with managed care companies and treatment providers

---

EAPs generally take one of five forms:

1. *Internal.* The internal program is staffed by a company employee who accepts both supervisor referrals and

self-referrals. He or she may conduct initial assessments, and frequently refers employees to community resources for counseling or treatment.

2. *External.* The external program is run by an outside agency that is under contract to provide most EAP services, including assessment.

3. *Labor union.* The labor union model is staffed by qualified union representatives and serves union members. Its primary service is referrals.

4. *Professional association.* The professional association program encourages members to use its services by controlling licensing. This option is used primarily by physicians, lawyers, and other licensed professionals.

5. *Consortia.* Small- or medium-sized companies that otherwise would not be able to afford to offer EAP service use the consortia. By joining several work populations into a single group, small businesses can contract with an EAP provider to deliver services at a quantity discount.

Drug Claims

The employee assistance program professional for a life insurance company headquartered in Philadelphia got a call late on a Friday afternoon from the regional manager of Cincinnati operations. He needed help. He had just been copied on a complaint filed by Dale, a twenty-year veteran of the claims processing department at the Cincinnati regional office. The complaint alleged that the department head was routinely stoned at work, made unreasonable— and often unethical—demands on staff, and could not manage the day-to-day responsibilities of his job. Citing specifics, Dale said that the department head instructed staff to "bury" claims that would be costly for the company to pay, fudge numbers on profitability reports, and lie to other department heads about his routine absences. Dale believed his boss was cheating innocent people out of insurance claims to which they were entitled because drugs had robbed him of his ability to make good judgments. It was a serious claim.

This was the first time that Dale had filed a complaint about any supervisor. Not one to make waves or point fingers, he acted out of desperation. The EAP professional recognized the significance of Dale's action. It's hard enough for most employees to break rank, harder yet to take an internal issue to the corporate level for resolution. The EAP professional moved into action quickly.

On Monday morning, she interviewed the other eleven members of the claims department by phone, without revealing the source of her concern. All but one, the newest member, corroborated Dale's observations. While all the others knew about the problem, most were hesitant to step forward out of fear of retaliation. The EAP professional reassured them that they would be supported in their efforts to resolve the problem. She then talked to other department heads at the Cincinnati office. They relayed other stories of bizarre or unprofessional behavior that intimated the presence of drugs or alcohol. The regional manager had been unaware of the problem because his contact with department heads was intermittent. He officed out of a different building.

Working in consort with the corporate human resources department and the regional manager, the EAP professional recommended that the company conduct a corporate intervention. At it, the department head would be offered an opportunity to receive a chemical dependency assessment and follow-up treatment as needed. To move things along, she identified an interventionist in the area who could facilitate. She also acted as a liaison between the insurance company, the interventionist, and the addicted department head—all from her office in Philadelphia.

The interventionist in turn used the EAP professional as a resource in the planning process. He tapped her for information on health insurance coverage, approved treatment providers, evidence of substance abuse, and history of prior addictions. She recommended potential intervention team members, based on her interviews and knowledge of the regional office. She also helped educate management on the need for intervention and received consensus on consequences if the intervention failed. Management agreed that if the department head refused treatment, he would forfeit his job.

The EAP professional did not attend this intervention but was pleased to learn that it was successful. The department head agreed to undergo treatment and took a six-month leave of absence. Before his return, the EAP professional helped develop an aftercare plan, and during his first year back, he continued to provide posttreatment accountability. The EAP professional played an invaluable role in returning the employee to peak productivity.

5

The Treatment Process

Every employer faced with drug or alcohol addiction in its ranks asks the same question: Does treatment really work? It's a legitimate concern. The value of the intervention process hinges on the effectiveness of treatment options. The honest answer is that treatment works, but not for all people and not always the first time. The following five factors have a positive impact on the outcome:

- High motivation
- Legal pressure to stay hospitalized
- No prior trouble with the law
- Psychological counseling while in treatment
- Lack of other psychological problems, especially antisocial personality disorders

These predictors of success were documented in a landmark study conducted in the early 1990s by the National Institute on Drug Abuse (NIDA). It followed the progress of more than 10,000 drug abusers in four different types of inpatient and outpatient treatment programs over the course of three years. The study validated what addiction counselors have known all along—that drug abuse treatment programs are effective in arresting the disease, regardless of the type of program used.[1] That's good news for employers who are willing to invest in treatment to get their employees healthy and productive again.

The clinical continuum of care charts the recovery process from start to finish, as shown below. It consists of three steps: (1) intervention, (2) primary treatment—either inpatient or outpatient, and (3) aftercare. Recovery is a lifelong endeavor.

Intervention: The First Step

Until ten years ago, intervention was not included on the care continuum. It was viewed as a stand-alone event that was foreign to treatment. It also carried a negative stigma because of its early reliance on shame as a motivator. This distancing attitude changed dramatically in the 1990s as interventions became more common and treatment centers had good results with intervened patients. Interventions now are a respected, integral part of the treatment process. Almost every reputable treatment center in the United States and around the world supports the concept.

The primary benefit of a successful intervention is that it gets an employee to a place where he or she can accept treatment. The secondary benefit is that it unearths volumes of information that can be beneficial to the treatment staff. Clinicians everywhere have come to appreciate the value of this insight. Like a great bumper sticker that finally comes out of the drawer, clinicians have stuck intervention on the front end of the continuum of care. The value of intervention insight goes beyond the initial assessment. It shapes the aftercare planning process, especially if the interventionist stays involved in a co-case management role. Acting as a liaison among the clinical staff, employer, and family, he or she has a unique perspective on the employee's situation and support network. The interventionist can bring that perspective to aftercare planning, which enhances the possibility of a successful recovery.

The medical profession's view of the intervention process isn't the only thing that's undergone a transformation in the last decade. Training requirements for interventionists have become more stringent and formal. Training has enabled them to make better assessments and recommendations. That translates into a better approach to treatment, and generally, better results. Accreditation programs and professional associations have elevated the level of professionalism across the board. The Association of Intervention Specialists developed the industry's first code of ethics in 1997. It requires all interventionists to uphold professional practice standards relating to confidentiality, boundaries, and intervention approach. It also encourages members to carry malpractice insurance, a practice which protects both clients and interventionists.

Figure 5-1: The Continuum of Care

The Old View

The New View

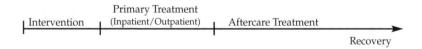

Family Members at Corporate Interventions

When contemplating an employee intervention, companies invariably face the question of whether to include family members on the intervention team. There is no simple answer. The presence of a family member can have a tremendous impact on the outcome of the intervention—positively or negatively.

In an ideal situation, one or two members of the employee's family are present. This happened in the design studio intervention that follows, "The Elephant in the Office," where the creative director's adult daughter joined the intervention team. Her participation was appropriate because she had a preexisting relationship with the studio. This is not always the case. In many organizations, staff members have no relationship with the addicted employee's family or friends and no way of knowing if anyone at home is concerned about the employee's substance abuse problem. It's possible that the employee's spouse or partner is engaged in the same detrimental lifestyle. If the spouse drinks or does drugs with the employee, he or she does not belong at the intervention. The opposite could be true, but the company has no way of knowing it. When in doubt, I always recommend erring on the cautious side. One misstep can botch the intervention.

Many times, corporate interventions are initiated by family members. A husband recognizes that his wife has a drinking problem and calls one of her friends at work for confirmation and advice. The friend agrees that there is a problem and seeks the confidential advice of the employee assistance profession or human resources manager. The HR manager calls in an interventionist, who in turn assembles the intervention team. The employee's husband, her friend, her office mate, and her boss participate in the meeting. This is technically a corporate intervention, but it began with a distress call from a family member.

Primary Treatment: The Second Step

The second step on the continuum of care is primary treatment. It begins when an employee is admitted into a treatment program. A trained clinician assesses his or her case and prescribes a personalized program that includes some kind of therapy with other people. There are many different kinds of primary treatment, each designed to meet the unique needs of the afflicted employee. They range from outpatient programs, where the employee attends each day or evening but still lives at home, to inpatient programs, where the employee stays in a clinic or hospital. Sometimes the treatment plan is a combination of both. Often, it centers around AA or another Twelve Step program.

Today's treatment style is considerably less confrontational than in the past. Treatment professionals realize that it's unnecessary, and often counterproductive, to use the old condescending, shaming approach. Patients respond better to a respectful, caring style that treats alcoholism and addiction as a no-fault disease. The days when an addicted employee sat in the middle of a treatment circle—in what used to be called "the hot seat"—to be confronted by peers and counselors are long gone.

Inpatient Programs

The inpatient program was the predominant method used to treat alcoholics and addicts through the 1980s. Originated in Minnesota, it's still the most widely used model of inpatient treatment in the country and has been duplicated around the world. The first inpatient program was developed in the 1950s at Willmar State Hospital in Willmar, Minnesota, and refined at Hazelden in Center City, a small community just north of Minneapolis and Saint Paul. One of the hallmarks of this "Minnesota Model" is that it treats the whole person—mind, body, and spirit. Its philosophy is rooted in values of respect and dignity.

Most inpatient programs last between twenty-one and thirty-two days. Many employers are surprised to learn that even short-term stays can yield significant declines in substance abuse. Length of stay is less an indicator of success than the employee's sincere desire to get better, and his or her access to professional counseling. Aftercare is developed about three weeks into treatment. Some employees need to stay in treatment longer than a month. This happens when the employee has a long history of drug or alcohol abuse and has tried several other times to get clean and sober without success. For them, one month in primary treatment is just not long enough. They have demonstrated through past behavior that they need an extended stay in a safe environment to establish a solid foundation for recovery. Although few chemical dependency treatment providers offer extended care options, a number of clinics and hospitals do. The normal length of time for long-term inpatient primary care is four to six months, not including the transition period into a structured aftercare setting, like a halfway house.

Inpatient programs offer a variety of therapeutic exercises and events throughout the treatment day. Some are required as part of the treatment plan, others are optional. Activities include individual counseling, lectures, group counseling, relaxation classes, reading time, Twelve Step meetings, exercise, and other physical activities. Although most incoming participants can't imagine what they will do to fill their time, their days are full. Most comment on how fast the time passes while they're in treatment.

Most inpatient programs in the United States use a multidisciplinary team approach to primary treatment. They pair the employee with a group of health care professionals, all of whom bring a unique perspective to the treatment process. A typical team might include the following:

- *Clinical case manager.* This person gets involved right from the beginning. He or she works with the interventionist, employee assistance program professional or family member in preparing the preadmission paperwork. The clinical case manager makes sure that a bed has been reserved, financial information is in place, the employee is cleared medically and psychologically, and any loose ends are tied up prior to admission. While this sounds tedious, it's important in ensuring a smooth transition from intervention to treatment. The last thing anyone needs after the intervention is to find out that the clinic is full and the employee has to be bumped to another program. The clinical case manager oversees this entire process and works with the treatment team throughout the employee's stay.

- *Primary counselor.* This professional provides the bulk of the employee's counseling while in treatment. The primary counselor has more face-to-face time with the employee than any other treatment team member. In many cases, he or she coordinates the involvement of the other professionals on the team. Because the primary counselor knows the employee more intimately, he or she plays an important role in the development of the employee's treatment.

- *Psychologist.* Most treatment programs provide psychological testing as part of the initial assessment. These tests provide insight into issues that may affect the employee's response to treatment—including depression levels, cognitive skills, and self-esteem. The staff psychologist conducts the tests and works closely with the staff psychiatrist or medical doctor in monitoring the employee throughout treatment. This involvement is important if the employee needs to take medication while in treatment. For example, if an employee were diagnosed with clinical depression during the preadmission assessment, he or she may begin taking antidepressants while in treatment. The medical staff would keep close tabs on the employee to make sure the dosage is correct and the medicine doesn't trigger any negative side effects.

- *Medical doctor or psychiatrist.* Most assessments begin with a physical exam administered by a medical doctor. This precautionary measure checks for medical conditions that might prevent the employee from fully participating in treatment. It also looks for possible withdrawal complications during detoxification. All medical conditions are carefully monitored throughout treatment. If the exam identifies any psychological or psychiatric issues that need to be addressed, the psychiatrist participates in the employee's treatment planning and ongoing medication management.

- *Family counselor.* The family counselor assesses the clinical needs of the employee's support system—namely family members and close friends. Sometimes co-workers are included in this list. It's his or her job to connect family members with support services that can aid in their healing process. This means coordinating schedules for the family program and facilitating family conferences, among other things. Alcoholism and addiction are family illnesses. They can play havoc on even the strongest family relationships. Most employees in treatment for chemical dependency suffer under the burden of strained family relationships. Ideally, the entire family can begin the healing process at the same time that the addicted employee does.

- *Clergy.* Spirituality plays an integral part of most addicts' treatment and recovery. Clergy who understand the deep emotional scars of this illness can help addicted employees forgive themselves and draw on their belief in a higher power to become whole again. Twelve Step programs like Alcoholics Anonymous put a lot of emphasis on the role of spirituality in the recovery process. Many employees in treatment remark on how much peace they found from reconnecting with a power greater than themselves. Others "fake it 'til they make it."

- *Aftercare specialist.* This person develops the aftercare plan for the employee to follow once he or she completes primary treatment. Drawing upon his or her network of recovery resources, the aftercare specialist can connect the employee to groups or programs that provide ongoing support during recovery. I view aftercare as step three in the recovery process. Without it, primary treatment can be an exercise in futility. Research supports my stance. Employees who participate in a structured aftercare program greatly enhance their chances of continued abstinence. Employees who isolate themselves and attempt to remain clean and sober on their own experience a high rate of relapse. This is discussed in more detail later in the chapter.

- *Recreational therapist.* Most practicing alcoholics or addicts do not have the motivation to participate in recreational activities while they are impaired. As a result, many are unfit. The recreational therapist assesses this dimension of employees' lives and recommends physical activities to rebuild strength, agility, and energy. He or she develops a balanced plan to integrate healthy activities and fun into their lives. Physical fitness coaching reflects the holistic treatment philosophy that approaches the mind, body, and spirit as inseparable dimensions of the whole.

- *Nutritionist.* It's normal to discover that addicted employees have not been eating healthy foods or recommended portions prior to entering treatment. Many have been substituting liquor for food, starting the day with a shot of whiskey instead of a spot of orange juice. The nutritionist helps them learn healthy eating habits while in treatment. Like exercise, good nutrition is vitally important to reclaiming good overall health.

OUTPATIENT PROGRAMS

Throughout the 1980s, the standard prescription for chemical dependency was a one-month stay at an inpatient treatment facility. Although many treatment centers still use this model successfully, there now are outpatient alternatives that can be just as effective.

Outpatient treatment has gained in popularity for several reasons. It is viewed as less expensive, less time-consuming, and more flexible than inpatient treatment—especially by insurance companies or managed care providers who pay the bill. They often make the final decision on whether the client receives intensive inpatient treatment or less-intensive outpatient treatment. This decision is based on both financial considerations and medical necessity. If an employee is not at risk for medical complications or physical withdrawal symptoms, the insurance company generally will not authorize inpatient treatment, unless the employee has failed many outpatient programs in the past. If the employee is in need of medical attention for detoxification, insurance sometimes will cover a limited inpatient stay followed by an immediate transition to an outpatient setting.

Outpatient treatment starts with an initial assessment and consists mostly of dynamic group therapy. Individual counseling is available if prearranged with the group leader. The length of outpatient programs can vary greatly from one provider to another. Programs usually last between six and twelve weeks, but can continue as long as six months. Like inpatient programs, they include an aftercare plan developed while the person is in treatment. Aftercare can last for a year after completion of the program.

When making choices between inpatient and outpatient tracks, it is critical to consider the psychological needs of addicted employees. They may not be suffering physically, but may be in terrible shape emotionally. Emotionally unstable employees will make better progress if they can wake up in treatment rather than drive to outpatient classes five times a week.

Outpatient treatment programs are extremely successful when employees are highly motivated. They have the discipline to self-regulate and the clarity of purpose to effectively manage their time. Unfortunately, most intervened employees don't fall into this gung ho camp. If they did, intervention would not have been necessary. Many are still grappling with a high degree of denial and are fighting the need for any kind of treatment. In my experience, they may not be the best candidates for outpatient treatment.

ADDICTION IS A FAMILY DISEASE

Any book about workplace addiction would be incomplete if it did not address the effects of the disease on the employee's family. After working closely with families of addicted employees for more than twenty years, I have seen the devastation that the illness can cause. Thankfully, I also have watched families overcome the disease and reclaim their lives, relationships, and happiness. One of the characteristics of untreated addiction is that it is extremely selfish and controlling. Like a spoiled child, it demands all the attention. Other members of the family, and other priorities, get neglected. Family members feel as though they are in competition with the illness for the addict's time, attention, personality, money, and more.

Family members who live with addiction can become as impaired as the alcoholic or addict. The disease takes over a household without family members even realizing it. One day they wake up and find an "elephant in the living room," a beast which everyone tiptoes around and no one acknowledges. I call this "the conspiracy of silence." Family members organize their lives around the disease. Healthy boundaries begin to blur. Everything about their lives and selves becomes enmeshed. This leads family members to wonder, "Where does he stop and I start?" They find themselves on an emotional roller coaster that's controlled by the addict. The engine sounds like this: "When you're okay, I'm okay. When you're happy, I'm happy. When you feel bad, I feel bad. When you're sad, I'm sad." The roller coaster makes the other family members sick. They forfeit their sense of self and harness their emotions to those of the addict. Distinctions among people disappear. These are the symptoms of codependency.

Codependency can infect an office as well as a home. Co-workers are just as vulnerable as family members to the invisible elephant syndrome, the employee's emotional spikes, and the floating boundaries of addiction. The major challenge in treating anyone close to the addict is helping him or her break free from the painful hold the disease has on his or her life. In some cases, there is a need for physical separation from the addicted employee. More often, an emotional separation will suffice. Family members, co-workers, and friends need to extract themselves to regain a sense of self. This is harder than it sounds. The employee will work hard to keep those around him or her engaged. Avoiding physical contact isn't always possible, so protective shields need to be erected.

The Elephant in the Office

A West Coast graphic design studio had grown from five employees to twenty-two in just two years. Its client list included Fortune 500 firms and a number of high-growth technology firms. Business was booming, but there was something holding the firm back. The staff was tense and edgy. Even when the workload was reasonable, they seemed to have short fuses and poor attitudes. A general sense of distress prevailed.

Charlie, the general manager, was perplexed. He asked the designers and production specialists what the problem was, but they couldn't seem to put their fingers on it. He queried the traffic manager and bookkeeper, but they were just as equivocal. Something was not right, but no one could identify the cause. No one except Karen, the office manager. She had grown up in an alcoholic family and recognized the symptoms right away.

Karen was a straightforward, take-charge type who didn't mince words. Everyone respected her ability to take on problems and find solutions. She told Charlie that the creative director had a problem with alcohol. Karen had smelled it on her breath in the mornings and when she came back from meetings. She had seen it in her manic behavior among the staff and with clients. Charlie pressed her for more information.

Pausing a moment to collect her emotions, Karen told Charlie that her father was an alcoholic for as long as she could remember. He drank every day until liver disease took his life when Karen was nineteen. What hit home was that office life was beginning to feel like home life before her dad died. Her mother had forbid any of the kids to talk about the drinking, hoping in vain that his problem would just go away. Karen learned from experience that alcoholism does not right itself, and it doesn't disappear of its own accord. The family tolerated her dad's tirades, and covered for his mistakes, but never acknowledged the cause—just like the staff was doing for the creative director. The elephant from her living room had taken up residence in the design studio, and everyone was pretending not to notice.

When Charlie asked if Karen was sure that alcoholism was the cause of the staff unrest, Karen identified behavior patterns that paralleled the erratic, confusing environment she had grown up in. Everyone started the day by checking the "temperature" or volatility in the office. Staff members were trying to detect if the creative director had been bingeing the night before, if she was drinking already that morning, if it would be okay to approach her about a layout before noon. They didn't want to upset her. The entire tone of the day was set by how she was faring.

The addict's extreme mood swings had erected an office roller coaster with twenty-two people strapped on board. Everyone just closed their eyes and took the plunge, even those with no stomach for emotional upheaval. Even Karen found herself reacting to her boss the way she'd reacted to her dad, something she'd vowed she would never do again. She urged Charlie to do something to address the drinking before it sent the staff ever the edge.

Charlie knew enough to go outside the firm to get professional advice. The interventionist worked with Karen, Charlie, and the creative director's adult daughter, who had previously expressed concern to staff members about her mother's drinking problem, to develop the intervention strategy. After taking the necessary planning steps, they held the meeting in the studio conference room after the close of business on a Friday. The creative director initially was stunned, but agreed to undergo treatment. She was admitted that evening.

At Charlie's request, the interventionist met with the staff the following week to educate them on the disease of addiction. The interventionist observed how much energy the members had spent trying in vain to sidestep their boss's alcoholism. He helped them set boundaries to protect themselves from being cast in enabling roles again.

The air in the office changed noticeably after the intervention. Energy was high and the mood upbeat. Despite the distraction of the intervention and the temporary absence of the creative director, the studio was productive. Everybody won—the staff, the clients, and the intervened employee. She came back to work a month later and thanked Karen for having the courage to confront the problem head on.

SETTING BOUNDARIES

Setting healthy boundaries for the co-workers, family, and friends of an intervened employee is an important part of intervention education. One concern is that the intervened employee may think that people no longer care about him or her because they are pulling away. "The

Language of Letting Go" helps make the distinction between caring *for* and caring *about* the addicted employee.

The Language of Letting Go
Author unknown

To let go doesn't mean to stop caring,
It means I can't do it for someone else.
To let go is not to cut myself off,
It's the realization that I can't control another.
To let go is not to enable,
But to allow learning from natural consequences.
To let go is to admit powerlessness,
Which means the outcome is not in my hands.
To let go is not to try to change or blame another,
I can only change myself.
To let go is not to care for,
But to care about.
To let go is not to fix,
But to be supportive.
To let go is not to judge,
But to allow another to be a human being.
To let go is not to be arranging all the outcomes,
But to let others affect their own outcomes.
To let go is not to be protective,
It is to permit another to face reality.
To let go is not to deny,
But to accept.
To let go is not to nag, scold, or argue,
But to search for my own shortcomings and to
    correct them.
To let go is not to adjust everything to my desires,
But to take each day as it comes.
To let go is not to criticize and regulate anyone,
But to try to become what I dream I can be.

To let go is not to regret the past,
But to grow and live for the future.

The poem explains how to avoid the destructive patterns of codependency. It gives co-workers and family members permission to disengage without feeling guilty or carrying the burden of the other person's disease. It's a prescription for becoming unmeshed. Families and co-workers who follow this path into recovery describe it as "freeing themselves from the bondage of this illness." The message here is that other people's recovery is not contingent on the addicted employee's recovery. It removes the old codependency crutch that says, "If you get better, I will get better." That mindset condemns all who follow it to a life of misery. If the addicted employee decides not to get better, no one around him or her is allowed to heal either. This kind of conditional thinking gives incredible power to the addict. No one deserves to have that much control over other people. Co-workers, family members, and friends need to know that they can recover regardless of the addict's decision.

IMPORTANCE OF FAMILY PROGRAMS

Almost all inpatient and outpatient treatment programs today address the codependency needs of family members. Family programs are important for two reasons. They help families recover from the ravages of the disease in ways they can't do on their own. And in healing the family, they create a healthier support system for employees in recovery. Long-term sobriety depends in part on a strong support network.

Family programs come in a rainbow of colors. At some inpatient treatment centers, families stay on campus and participate in full-day family treatment programs. At others, families stay off campus and commute to the facility for classes. Most outpatient treatment centers now offer opportunities for family involvement. Some provide family programs even if the addicted employee is not in treatment. There also are stand-alone inpatient codependency programs that have no direct connection with primary chemical dependency programs. These are extremely effective for families who have no plans to intervene but desperately need help for themselves. One example is the Caron Foundation's freestanding family codependency program.

There was a significant shift in family treatment philosophies between the 1970s and 1980s. Many centers moved from what I describe as "patient-centered" to "family-centered" treatment programs. The feeling among care providers was that the alcoholic or addicted employee was receiving attention from the primary treatment clinical team, but the family was being neglected. They understood that family members had been profoundly affected by this painful illness. They believed that families would benefit from the opportunity to receive proper clinical help.

The thrust of family programs falls into three broad clusters: awareness and education, fellowship with other families, and the beginning of healthy communications.

- *Awareness and education.* First and foremost, family programs teach the family of an addicted employee what the disease is really all about. This alone can be a source of great relief and open the gates of healing. In understanding the disease, family members can make sense of the chaos and insanity of their lives as manifestations of the illness. They can take comfort in the realization that they are not crazy. Alcohol and drug addiction is a crazy-making disease. It's normal for family members to feel guilty or responsible for the addict's problems and pain. They think the problems must be their fault, telling themselves that if only they had acted differently or changed in some way, the employee would not drink or use drugs. This shaming refrain is reinforced by the impaired person blaming family members for his or her dilemma. The family program helps them understand that they cannot be responsible for another person.

- *Fellowship with other families.* There is a healing element to people sharing a common problem and similar experiences. This communion of grief has a positive effect on family members, not unlike what happens when alcoholics and addicts get together in a spirit of recovery. The common bond of pain and suffering brings people closer in an effort to help one another. The process enables family members to overcome isolation, one of the destructive side effects of the disease. It helps them put a voice to their feelings, an exercise that can be very cathartic. It's difficult to explain to outsiders just what insanity they have been experiencing, so they tend to clam up. It's easier and safer not to air the family laundry. What a relief it is for them to learn that they are not alone in their struggle against the disease.

- *Healthy communications.* Family programs enable members to begin discussing family issues in a safe place, with the help of a counselor or family therapist. For many, this open communication is a first. The facilitator prevents any blaming or inappropriate talk among family members and the employee. They all learn new ways of relating to each other, skills they can take home when they finish treatment. Healthy communication is made possible because the addicted person is sober and more emotionally stable. Just as important, family members are more informed about the dynamics of the disease and more practiced in positive communication techniques.

The primary treatment counselor helps decide which subjects are most appropriate to cover in family sessions. He or she has been involved in the employee's treatment from the beginning and has a sense of what the family needs to address. He or she also knows when it's the right time to open a topic. It's counterproductive to rush into some issues—such as alcohol-related abuse or financial struggles—before the family is ready. Some things need to wait until home life settles down and the family begins to heal.

Although co-workers don't attend family treatment programs, they sometimes have access to company-sponsored education programs on addiction and recovery. They also can participate in any number of "concerned persons" support groups sponsored by area clinics and other organizations devoted to helping non-addicts break free from the web of addiction. The most recognized recovery program for families, co-workers, and friends of alcoholics and addicts is Al-Anon. Like Alcoholic Anonymous, after which it's patterned, Al-Anon is a Twelve Step program that encourages participants to further their recovery by attending weekly support meetings. There's more about this subject later in this chapter.

Aftercare: The Third Step

The idea that treatment "fixes" an addicted employee for good is widely held in corporate circles. This faulty expectation sets up everyone for disappointment, especially the recovering employee. Treatment is only one part of the recovery process. It doesn't profess to cure employees, only to help them manage their illness. No one is ever *cured* of alcoholism or addiction. What is reasonable to expect is that the disease can be arrested if the employee undergoes all three steps in the recovery process — intervention, primary care, and aftercare. Of the three, aftercare is the most important to long-term success. That's why treatment centers go to the effort of mapping it out. They understand how critical it is to recovery. In my experience, an employee's chances of remaining clean and sober for one year or longer after treatment *with the support of an aftercare program* are as high as 80 percent. *Without the support of an aftercare program*, the chances drop off dramatically.

The disease of alcoholism and addiction centers in the mind, not the bottle or drug. Recovery would be infinitely easier if alcohol or drugs were the problem. Remove the chemical and the problem would disappear. Treatment would consist of three-day detoxification centers. There would be no need for primary care or aftercare. Unfortunately, the disease does not work that way. How an addict uses chemicals is only a symptom of a multifaceted, debilitating disease that invades all dimensions of the body. The real work of recovery starts once the employee gets clean and sober. Only then is it possible to resolve underlying issues such as low self-esteem, honesty, and depression.

Aftercare programs can vary greatly, depending on the employee's history and what he or she does in recovery. Aftercare recommendations are clinically driven and fit one of three levels of involvement. The most intensive level is a continuation of primary treatment, called "extended care." It reflects the need for more time to address unresolved issues in a safe, structured setting. The next level transitions the recovering employee from a primary treatment setting to a halfway house. This "sober living environment" gives the employee an opportunity to live in a sober place, with sober people, while making the shift to a new way of life. In some cases, the employee may work during the day if he or she demonstrates a willingness to maintain sobriety. The third level of aftercare combines psychotherapy and Twelve Step meeting attendance. This is the most prevalent.

The common denominator in most aftercare plans is regular attendance in a Twelve Step program. The oldest and most widely known is Alcoholics Anonymous (AA). Since its inception more than sixty years ago, many other groups have adapted, with great success, the original Twelve Step model to such addictions as gambling, cocaine, sex, and narcotics. These organizations offer employees in recovery an opportunity to connect with other people suffering from the same obsession. This mutual support is essential to ongoing sobriety. For that reason, I highly recommend that every employee in recovery attend weekly Twelve Step support group meetings. The Twelve Step program has been effective in more than 150 countries. While there are other recovery options available, none has proven to be as effective. A word of caution: The true gauge of how well an employee is doing in recovery is not to be judged at AA meetings or counseling sessions. It's based on how he or she acts in three day-to-day settings—the office, the living room, and the freeway.

6

Legal Issues of Addiction

The legal ramifications of workplace addiction terrify some managers, baffle others, and go unnoticed by others. Those who dread a legal backlash are often paralyzed into inaction. Those who are slaves to the law unnecessarily complicate their lives. Those who pay no heed to the legal pitfalls expose themselves and their companies to potential lawsuits through ill-considered firings or job assignments. Whichever way they lean, employers of every size would be well served to understand the legal issues surrounding addiction. In today's litigious environment, they need to know how to walk the tightrope between helping addicted employees reclaim their lives and protecting the company and other employees from liability and risk.

A national survey of employers recently found that nearly 30 percent of employers would immediately terminate employees who displayed alcohol or drug-related behavior on the job.[1] This response is ill advised. First, it may be illegal to fire an employee just because he or she is an alcoholic or drug addict. Second, it may be short-sighted. Employers need to consider the challenges of attracting and retaining qualified employees in this era of low unemployment before writing off someone who could bring value to the company in recovery. Abrupt firings have both legal and bottom-line implications that often are overlooked.

Most managers have little training in the area of employment law. They lack the knowledge or experience to make informed decisions. They forget that by focusing on employee behavior or performance, they often can avoid legal issues altogether. Add to the knowledge gap the fact that workplace addiction is rarely a black-and-white issue, and confusion reigns. Legal issues surrounding workplace addiction take on varying casts of gray, depending on the situation, the employee's work history, the company's personnel policies, changing legal precedents, and other muddying factors. This chapter explores the legal gray zone of chemical dependency in the workplace. It's intended to give managers confidence in maneuvering through the maze of legal requirements. It offers general guidance on compliance, not unequivocal legal advice. For questions on specific cases, they should consult corporate counsel.

The Americans with Disabilities Act

Managers need to have a working knowledge of the Americans with Disabilities Act (ADA). It "prohibits private employers, state and local governments, employment agencies, and labor unions from discriminating against qualified individuals with disabilities in job application procedures, hiring, firing, advancement, compensation, job training, and other terms, conditions, and privileges of employment." The ADA makes it clear that an individual with alcoholism or drug addiction has a disability, and that this disability is protected under the law. It is not, however, an open license to use. Nor does it apply to all employees who exhibit signs of substance abuse in the workplace—only those who have been clinically diagnosed as addicted. This diagnosis requirement puts managers in a difficult place. They must walk the fine line between enforcing performance standards for all employees, including those suspected of substance abuse, while making reasonable accommodations for employees with documented addiction disabilities.

The act was signed into law on July 26, 1990. The U.S. Equal Employment Opportunity Commission issued regulations to enforce the provisions exactly a year later, and the law took effect on that same date in 1992. The law provides guidelines for both employers and employees to follow. The original statute covered employers with twenty-five or more employees. In 1994, this threshold dropped to include employers with fifteen or more employees.[2]

The ADA is divided into five main titles covering employment, public services, public accommodations, telecommunications, and miscellaneous provisions. Title I applies to all aspects of employment and covers employees disabled by addiction in the workplace.[3]

The Five Titles of the ADA

Title I: Employment. Employers must provide reasonable accommodations to individuals with disabilities to enable them to perform their job duties. Possible accommodations may include restructuring jobs, altering the layout of workstations, modifying equipment, and alterations in the application process. Medical examinations are highly regulated.

Title II: Public Services. Public services that include state and local government instrumentalities, the National Railroad Passenger Corporation, and other commuter authorities cannot deny services to people with disabilities participating in programs or activities that are available to people without disabilities. In addition, public transportation systems, such as public transit buses, must be accessible to individuals with disabilities.

Title III: Public Accommodations. All new construction and modifications must be accessible to individuals with disabilities. For existing facilities, barriers to services must be removed if readily achievable. Public accommodations include facilities such as restaurants, hotels, grocery stores, retail stores, etc., as well as privately owned transportation systems.

Title IV: Telecommunications. Telecommunications companies offering telephone service to the general public must have a telephone relay service to individuals who use telecommunication devices for the deaf (TTYs) or similar devices.

Title V: Miscellaneous. This includes a provision prohibiting either coercing, threatening, or retaliating against persons with disabilities or those attempting to aid persons with disabilities who assert their rights under the ADA.

The ADA defines an individual with a disability as someone who "has a physical or mental impairment that substantially limits one at more major life activities; has a record of such an impairment; or is regarded as having such an impairment."[4] Note that the language lists the person first and the disability second. This is the preferred nomenclature because it recognizes the existence of the individual apart from his or her disability. There's one further point about word choices. Employers should never refer to an employee suspected of substance abuse as an alcoholic or addict. Only qualified health care diagnosticians are allowed to make that determination.

The ADA definition means that employees who are alcoholics or addicts—or recovering alcoholics or addicts—are covered under the ADA, since addiction, by definition, significantly interferes with at least one major area of their lives. In considering the impact on life activities, recall that employees who stop using drugs or alcohol are never "cured" of the disease. They simply move into a suspended state of "recovery."

The ADA addresses three major areas of interest to managers: hiring, employment accommodations, and termination.

ADA Hiring Issues

On the issue of hiring, the ADA defines a qualified employee or applicant with a disability as someone who, with or without reasonable accommodation, can perform the essential functions of the job. Most of the time, however, managers don't know that an applicant has a disability related to drug or alcohol abuse. Addiction is not easily recognizable in a job interview. When they do know about a previous drug or alcohol addiction, employers frequently refuse to hire the candidate—despite ADA protections against discrimination. A 1999 telephone survey asked businesspeople which candidate they would hire: a person who is not a recovering alcoholic or addict, or a person with the same qualifications who is recovering from alcohol or drug addiction.[5] The poll found that almost half would choose the non-recovering candidate. This bias reflects a widespread lack of awareness of the strengths of people in recovery. My experience suggests that people in recovery make excellent, loyal employees who bring an appreciation to the job that's rare and valuable. People who have not been where they've been, and come back, don't share the same enthusiasm for life, opportunities, and relationships. I caution employers not to write off candidates in recovery without due consideration.

ADA Accommodations

The question of reasonable accommodations usually doesn't surface until after someone has been on the job for a while, and only after he or she has been clinically diagnosed as having a disability covered by the ADA. The law describes reasonable accommodation as

- making existing facilities used by employees readily accessible to and usable by persons with disabilities
- restructuring jobs, modifying work schedules, or reassigning to a vacant position
- acquiring or modifying equipment or devices; adjusting or modifying examinations, training materials, or policies; and providing qualified readers or interpreters

Reasonable accommodation for people with addictions, may include periodic drug or alcohol testing, counseling, modifying job responsibilities or increased supervision. In general, it would be reasonable to expect an employer to grant an employee an unpaid leave of absence to attend treatment. (Note: Up to twelve weeks of medical leave are guaranteed under the Family and Medical Leave Act for employees who have worked at least 1,250 hours in the previous twelve months.) It probably also would be reasonable to extend that leave by a month or two if an employee needed extended care. It would be reasonable to allow an employee to work a 7 A.M. to 4 P.M. schedule to be able to attend evening Twelve Step meetings. It probably would not be reasonable to ask the employer to release the employee every afternoon at 2 P.M. for AA meetings, especially if evening meetings were an option.

Another example may be helpful. A delivery person who is convicted of driving while under the influence (DWI) typically would not be allowed to continue the same job. He or she would pose a risk to the public, the company, and customers. Instead of terminating the employee, the company could attempt to reassign him or her to another open position. This could be packing boxes in the warehouse or dispatching other drivers—anything that does not involve the operation of potentially dangerous machinery or motorized vehicles.

While the ADA requires employers to make reasonable accommodation for alcoholics, it never requires an employer to tolerate problem behaviors related to alcohol abuse or substandard performance resulting from alcohol use or alcoholism. In fact, the law specifically provides that employers may prohibit alcohol in the workplace, require employees to be free from the influence of alcohol at work, and require the same job performance and behavior from employees with alcoholism as other employees. In addition, the ADA affords no protection to employees who formerly used drugs or are in recovery from drug abuse. It also excludes tests for illegal drugs from ADA restrictions on medical examinations. In all cases, it empowers employers to hold alcoholics and illegal drug users to the same performance standards as other employees.[6] In reality, managers often hold recovering alcoholics and addicts to a higher standard of performance than other employees. Their actions are motivated by fear that the recovering employee might relapse and cycle back into problematic behavior. Sometimes, the opposite is true. A manager accepts a lower standard of performance from a recovering employee as a means of avoiding confrontation or being "supportive." The line between "reasonable accommodation" and "substandard behavior" can be difficult to gauge.

ADA TERMINATION ISSUES

The topic of terminating an alcoholic employee is murkier. An employer may exclude an individual on the basis of alcoholism—even though that person would normally be protected under the ADA—if the employer can demonstrate either of the following:

- The exclusion is "job related and consistent with the business necessity." (This proposition is subject to debate. The Equal Employment Opportunity Commission [EEOC], which enforces the ADA, says that an individual must meet a higher "direct threat" rather than a lesser "business necessity" requirement. The one court that has addressed this issue rejected the EEOC view in favor of the "business necessity" view. The disagreement is over whether an employer can have a blanket policy or must make case-by-case determinations.[7]) The requirement means the individual cannot perform the essential functions of the job with or without reasonable accommodation. Using the example of a recovering alcoholic who is prone to blackouts, that candidate would not be suitable for a job as a pilot. Federal regulations and safety considerations make navigating a plane an impossibility. No amount of accommodation can outweigh the business necessity of mental alertness.

- The individual poses a risk to the health or safety of others, *and* that risk cannot be reduced below that level through reasonable accommodation. Consider an employee who has a history of physical violence when deprived of alcohol for more than a few hours. Clearly, the employer cannot permit the employee to drink on the job to reduce the possibility of violence. Nor can the company take the chance that the employee will strike out at a co-worker or customer out of frustration.

An untreated alcoholic or addict can create an unstable or unsafe workplace. Prudent employers address such risk head on—either by moving the employee into treatment, or removing him or her from payroll. In weighing the alternatives, employers need to remember three things. The first is that they are not qualified to diagnose an addiction. Only a trained clinician can make this determination. Until an employee has been clinically diagnosed with an addiction, the manager is not bound by the rules of the ADA. The second is that their decisions should be grounded in fact and related to the employee's actions, performance, and conduct. Managers should resist the inclination to assume things that are unproven or rely on negative stereotypes. They should also avoid the "what if" trap, which leads them to make rash decisions on the supposition that an employee will follow the same patterns of behavior as other employees with histories of substance abuse. The factual approach will minimize potential gray areas that might be fodder for a legal challenge by the employee. The third is that employees who have a history of alcoholism or addiction need an opportunity to receive treatment. If they refuse the offer, the employer may lawfully discharge them—assuming they are not meeting the expectations of their job. If they accept the offer and move into recovery, the employer retains a valuable, contributing employee.

Writing a Drug and Alcohol Policy

Every employer should have a written drug and alcohol policy that reflects the law and the values of the organization. The reasons are compelling. First, a well-crafted written policy sends a consistent message to all employees at every level. This lessens the opportunity for misunderstanding and confusion. Second, a written policy gives the company a firm platform on which to act if it does

encounter drug or alcohol problems and decides to intervene. Third, the process of writing the policy creates
buy-in among the staff ultimately charged with communicating and enforcing it.

Any drug and alcohol policy must comply with applicable state and federal laws and be understandable to
every person in the company. It also must fit the culture
of the organization. There is no formulaic approach, but
there are valuable models. The World Health Organization's (WHO) charter on alcohol in the workplace is
one. The charter embraces the principle that all people
should have "a family, community, and working life protected from accidents, violence, and other negative consequences of alcohol consumption."[8]

The Department of Labor recommends that any drug
and alcohol policy address five topics: (1) a written policy
statement; (2) supervisor training; (3) employee education and awareness; (4) employee assistance services;
and (5) drug and alcohol testing programs.[9] To be meaningful, a policy needs to be customized to match the
unique needs of the business, industry, employee mix,
and legal parameters. An airline, for example, may im-
pose requirements on pilots to ensure flight safely,
which a warehouse storage facility may not.

1. *Written policy.* This document explains the need for a
   drug and alcohol policy, the company's position on
   drug and alcohol use, and the consequences if an employee violates the policy. Policies differ among businesses and industries. Each needs to be drafted to
   reflect the needs, values, and issues of a particular
   business. It is often helpful to conduct an independent
   needs assessment prior to writing the policy.

2. *Supervisor training.* Training underpins the overall
   success of the program. Supervisors need to be able to

explain the policy to line employees as well as identify possible signs of abuse. To be effective in the dual role, they must not only understand the policy, they must endorse it. If supervisors are not comfortable with the policy, or do not see a need for it, they can thwart any efforts on the company's part to protect the safety of its workforce.

3. *Employee education and awareness.* To be effective, the policy must be readily understood and followed by the organization's employees. Without this understanding, the policy is just words on paper. It loses any power to affect change, influence behavior, or make employees feel safer in their work environment. There's no point in a company going through the work and expense of developing such a policy if it doesn't make the employees aware of it.

4. *Employee assistance services.* Confidential employee assistance programs (EAPs) are a cost-effective way for companies to help employees address personal issues, including substance abuse, that interfere with their work life. Such programs complete the cycle of addiction resolution—setting a substance abuse policy, identifying violations, and offering affected employees help. EAPs offer a variety of solutions, from short-term counseling to referrals to other health professionals in the community. Even smaller organizations can provide these services—by engaging an outside EAP contractor, participating in an EAP consortium, or simply referring employees to available community services. Often, such programs are covered by employee health insurance or other benefit programs.

5. *Drug and alcohol testing programs.* Drug testing conveys a message of zero tolerance for chemicals in the workplace. It adds teeth to any substance abuse policy, but

is not a substitute for a comprehensive policy or a panacea in the prevention of substance abuse. This is especially true if the drug testing program is the only measure in place. It easily can degenerate into a cat and mouse game where employees continue to use chemicals and simply try to trick the system.

Many companies tell employees of their drug and alcohol policy *only* at the time of hire. A recent poll found that almost one-third of employers follow this practice.[10] This defeats the point of having a policy. Even when employees know about the policy, they need to be reminded of its content. Policy statements, like personnel manuals and insurance documents, are filed and forgotten. To be effective, they should be circulated from time to time, talked about at in-service meetings, or highlighted periodically in company newsletters or memoranda. Employees also benefit from reminders of wellness and support resources available to them through the human resource department and employee assistance programs.

Drug-Free Workplace Act

Another useful model in drafting a drug and alcohol policy is the federal Drug-Free Workplace Act.[11] It requires any company with government contracts or grants to maintain a drug-free workplace or lose those contracts for up to five years. "Drug-free" means that no employee is allowed to use, make, sell, or distribute drugs at work. While the law governs only select businesses, its provisions benefit any business. Employers also should be mindful of state laws and regulations regarding drug and alcohol testing.

The Drug-Free Workplace Act requires businesses to inform employees of the dangers of drugs in the workplace and tell them that help is available. It specifically prohibits the use of controlled substances, including marijuana, co-caine, heroin, and hallucinogens. It also bans the use of some drugs that are not illegal—as long as the employee has a valid prescription—but are considered dangerous when used on the job. These include alcohol, ampheta-mines, and sedatives. A brief description of these chemi-cals is listed in the chemical guide at the back of the book.

If an employee is convicted of a workplace violation, the employer may either discipline that employee, which may include discharge, or offer to help combat the drug abuse problem. Help can take the form of counseling or a treatment program. If the employee refuses to accept as-sistance or fails to complete the agreed upon program, he or she risks termination. Under the act, employees must report workplace drug violations within five days of being convicted. They are not compelled to report viola-tions that happen outside of work.

Substance abuse issues in the workplace are rarely one-dimensional. They often coexist with other conditions, in-cluding mental health. This area is covered by the Mental Health Parity Act of 1996. Distinct from the ADA or Drug-Free Workplace Act, this act provides equal benefits for mental conditions as compared to physical conditions. While substance abuse and chemical dependency are not covered under the Mental Health Parity Act, coexisting mental health conditions may be.[12]

An Expensive Lesson

Maurie was vice president of merchandising for a trendy clothing manufacturing company in New York. He liked his job and had proven himself to be a talented manager of people and profits. His one nemesis was drinking. The more it escalated, the more his interactions with staff be-came strained and his performance plummeted. Com-plaints about excessive drinking and obnoxious behavior filtered in from retail clients as well. When sales numbers fell substantially below projections for the third straight quarter, the president took notice.

He talked to Maurie about his poor performance and objectionable conduct, but nothing improved. After consulting with his HR director and corporate counsel, he decided to retain an interventionist to address the drinking problem directly. The interventionist assembled a team and invited Maurie's wife, who had supported Maurie in an outpatient treatment program two years earlier, to participate.

Maurie was given the choice of a month-long inpatient treatment program or immediate dismissal. The interventionist explained that this was a last-chance offer. Maurie admitted that he had a drinking problem and agreed to return to treatment. At the company's urging, he signed an agreement stating that he would meet the expectations of the treatment and aftercare program as a condition of his continued employment. As a show of good faith, Maurie also signed a release-of-information form. It authorized the treatment center staff to discuss his progress with the interventionist, who served as a liaison among the company, the center, and Maurie's wife.

Maurie exceeded the staff's expectations while in treatment and was given an excellent prognosis for recovery. He was discharged on day twenty-nine and returned to work after spending a few days with his wife. On his first morning back, the president and HR director invited him to go out for lunch. He read the gesture as a congratulatory one, having successfully completed treatment. Instead, they fired him. It was a rash, punitive act designed to punish him for being an alcoholic. They viewed him as a "bad guy," not a "sick guy." He was permitted to go back to his office, under supervision, to collect his personal items.

Maurie was shocked. He had done everything that had been asked of him and assumed that his professional life would pick up where it had left off. That was the agreement. He left the meeting without touching his food and went home to break the news to his wife. Two weeks later, he filed suit. After months of deliberations, the court ordered the company to pay him $750,000 in damages for breach of contract and wrongful termination.

Confidentiality Laws

Maurie had agreed to release information about his progress in treatment to his employer as part of a last-chance agreement. However, the information could not have been released without his prior written authorization. The decision to sign information release authorization forms was entirely his. If he had refused, his privacy would have been protected by federal law. There are few exceptions to this law. This vigilant privacy protection can be difficult for employers to understand. It's based on the notion that alcoholics and drug addicts are more likely to receive help if they know their treatment is confidential.

Federal alcohol and drug confidentiality regulations "restrict the disclosure and use of patient-identifying information about individuals in substance abuse treatment. Patient-identifying information is information that reveals that a person is receiving, has received, or has applied for substance abuse treatment. The regulations do not protect the individual's identity per se, but rather his or her identity as a participant in or applicant for substance abuse treatment."[13] The regulations apply to holders, recipients, and seekers of patient-identifying information. Violators are subject to a criminal fine of up to $500 for the first offense and up to $5,000 for each subsequent offense. Violators also risk losing their state license to practice.

It is legal to transfer information to authorized persons if the patient/employee has signed the proper release form. Such a form must state the details of the information to be released with as much specificity as possible. To be valid, the consent form must include the information in the sample below.

Sample Consent Form

Patient name_____

Name of the program making the disclosure_____

_____

Purpose of the disclosure_____

_____

Name of person receiving the information_____

_____

Information to be released or received_____

_____

The patient understands that he or she may revoke the consent at any time, except to the extent that action has been taken in reliance on it. This consent form may be revoked orally or in writing.

Date or condition upon which the consent expires (if it has not been revoked earlier)_____

_____

Date of signature_____

Employee signature_____

With proper consent, the recipient of the release form may disclose information regarding the employee to outsiders, such as employers or relatives. There are three situations when patient-identifying information may be disclosed without patient consent: (1) the patient is threatening to commit a crime or hurt himself or others; (2) there is a medical emergency or child abuse or neglect is involved; and (3) a court order mandates disclosure, if the appropriate steps and procedures are taken.

When dealing with any issue relating to substance abuse in the workplace, employers can sidestep legal entanglements by focusing on performance and behavior. When legal issues do arise, they should err on the side of caution. Before contemplating any action related to hiring, discipline, accommodations or termination, it's wise to consult the ADA laws governing employees with disabilities, the Mental Health Parity Act covering employees with mental health conditions, the Drug-Free Workplace Act (if they have government contracts), and their own alcohol and drug abuse policy. They also are well advised to consult with an attorney who specializes in employment law. Every situation is unique, and different laws may apply in each case.

7

Other Addictions and Depression

For most of the past thirty years, people have used the clinical process of crisis intervention mostly for helping alcoholics and drug addicts. However, the process's role has greatly expanded in the past decade to include other addictions and mental health issues. Clinicians throughout the country conduct interventions for compulsive gambling, eating disorders, computer addiction, work addiction, sexual addiction, and more. As in the case of alcohol and drug addictions, the employee's problem is not the chemical, dice, food, computer, job, or sex. It's the disease of addiction. The same intervention framework that's used for chemical addictions works for these pathologies as well. They all share the common denominator of addiction: denial. They all benefit from raising the bottom through early intervention.

Depression

DEPRESSION AND SUBSTANCE ABUSE

Why would a book on chemical addiction in the workplace address depression? Approximately 60 percent of Americans in treatment for chemical dependency also suffer from clinical depression. Depression coexists with drug and alcohol addiction more frequently than any other mental illness. When the two diseases go hand in hand, they're a deadly combination. One cannot be effectively treated without addressing the other.

Clinical depression strikes employees of all races, economic groups, and professions. It causes them to lose motivation, energy, and interest in day-to-day work and life. Like substance abuse, depression is life threatening. Fortunately, it is readily treatable once diagnosed. Treatment for depression has made great strides in the last decade, thanks to a new generation of nonaddictive medications. They are highly effective but no longer slow down physical and cognitive responses the way early remedies did. Better yet, they work quickly. Employees on antidepressants feel better within weeks.

The most difficult thing about treating depression is diagnosing it, especially when it's paired with substance abuse. Many of the symptoms of substance abuse can mimic or mask the symptoms of depression, which are listed on page 146 under "Ten Symptoms of Depression." They are easily missed, even by professional assessors at drug and alcohol treatment centers. The more obvious disease of addiction overshadows the silent enemy of depression. It goes unnoticed. It doesn't matter which illness came first, or which is primary or secondary. For the employee to become healthy and productive again, both need to be recognized and treated. When depression goes undiagnosed, it becomes a strong relapse trigger for recovering employees. Although they successfully complete treatment, they still feel emotionally down. Many gravitate back to alcohol or drugs—a form of self-medication—just to feel normal or happy again.

The Magnitude of Workplace Depression

Depression affects more than nineteen million Americans each year, making it the most serious mental illness in the United States. Between 5 and 10 percent of the population—and the workforce—experience an episode of major depression each year.[1] In spite of its prevalence, depression is not on the radar screens of corporate America. One reason is that the financial toll of workplace depression is less than that of addiction. The bigger price tag attracts more attention. Depression also carries the stigma of mental illness, which discourages open disclosure or discussion. Employees are uncomfortable admitting to co-workers or supervisors that they suffer from a disease of the mind. It just doesn't play well in the world of work. Finally, most employers have at best a sketchy idea of what depression is or how much it siphons off the U.S. economy each year. If they were better informed, they likely would devote more resources to identifying and treating it among employees.

The National Mental Health Association estimates that depression costs American businesses $43 million a year in absenteeism, lost productivity, and the direct costs of treatment and rehabilitation. These estimates are understated because most cases go undetected and untreated. No one knows with certainty the magnitude of the illness in the workplace.

Cost of Workplace Depression[2]
- $43 billion dollars in annual costs in the United States
- $12 billion for treatment and rehabilitation
- $23 billion in absenteeism and lost productivity
- $7 billion in lost earnings due to depression-caused suicide

---

Research suggests that women are significantly more susceptible to depressive disorders than men. While the causes are still under investigation, some studies found a high correlation between stress and depression. Women, especially working women with families, tend to be under a lot of stress. Another study suggests that men are under-represented in the statistics because they have a more difficult time stepping forward to ask for help. The National Institute of Mental Health found that nearly twice as many women than men (12 percent versus 7 percent) are affected by depression each year. At some point in her life, one in every five women has an episode of depression that warrants treatment. A 1994 First Chicago study that tracked 18,000 employees found that eight out of ten employees affected by depression were women between the ages of twenty-seven and forty-six.[3] This is a red flag for any business with a predominantly female workforce.

Employees who are clinically depressed and go untreated can pose a risk to everyone in the workplace, including themselves. They are more prone to costly or dangerous mistakes due to lack of concentration. Depressed employees also have a higher propensity for physical violence, both at home and work. In reported incidents of workplace violence, the perpetrator frequently demonstrated signs of clinical depression prior to acting out. The risk of violence escalates if the employee suffers from both depression and substance abuse.

In severe cases, depressed employees will attempt to take their own lives. An estimated 30,000 Americans die each year from suicide. The actual fatality rate is probably twice as high because the cause of death often is misclassified. And while not every case of undiagnosed depression ends in suicide, many have serious consequences.

UNDERSTANDING DEPRESSION

The disease of depression is widely misunderstood, both on the work front and in the community. Many employers interpret depression as a sign of weak mindedness, much as they view addiction. The reality is that depression, like addiction, is caused by a chemical imbalance in the brain. It cannot be started or stopped by the employee who is afflicted. To be arrested, it must be professionally treated—most often with a combination of antidepressants and psychotherapy. Employers also make the mistake of equating depression with feeling down or blue. Clinical depression is much different than having a bad day, something everyone experiences now and again. Employees who experience true clinical depression describe it as an overwhelming feeling of hopelessness. Regardless of what's happening on the outside, they don't feel good on the inside. This abiding sadness can become so oppressive that they become incapacitated. It drives them to drop out of the workforce, act out in violent ways, have a mental breakdown, or attempt suicide.

Too often, evidence of untreated depression doesn't surface until crisis erupts. Society accepts depression as an underlying cause of mental breakdowns and suicide, but it hasn't reconciled itself to treating the cause or preventing the crisis. This disconnect creates a trap for the businesspeople suffering from depression. How can they get help when the system doesn't recognize the existence of their affliction? For them to acknowledge their depression is to appear unfit to perform their jobs. For people who define themselves by what they do, this is an untenable position. They often choose silence over self-disclosure as a means of preserving their position and their self-worth. They lose themselves in the process.

The National Institute of Mental Health has broken clinical depression into three types, each with its own distinct characteristics.[4] The list is presented to help employees and managers recognize the possible signs of depression, not diagnose the disease. Only a trained clinician can make that determination.

- *Major depression.* This type of depression is episodic, with each episode lasting about two weeks. Episodes can recur throughout an employee's lifetime. Major depression exists when at least five or more of the symptoms of depression are present.
- *Dysthymia.* This is a less severe yet more chronic form of depression. It is diagnosed when the depressed mood persists for at least two years in adults or one year in children or adolescents. Many employees with dysthymic disorder also experience episodes of major depression.
- *Bipolar disorder.* The bipolar employee alternates between episodes of major depression and periods of mania or abnormally high moods. These polar opposites combine with at least three of the following symptoms: overly inflated self-esteem, decreased need for sleep, increased talkativeness, racing thoughts, distractibility, increased goal-directed activity, physical agitation, and excessive involvement in pleasurable activities that have a high potential for painful consequences.

Ten Symptoms of Depression[5]

1. Persistent sad, anxious, or empty mood
2. Loss of interest or pleasure in activities that used to be enjoyed
3. Persistent physical symptoms that don't respond to treatment
4. Irritability or edginess for no apparent reason
5. Changes in sleep patterns—trouble falling asleep or sleeping too much
6. Inability to concentrate, remember things, or make decisions

7. Weight gain or loss, or change in appetite
8. Chronic fatigue or loss of energy
9. Feelings of guilt, hopelessness, or worthlessness
10. Thoughts of suicide or death

Recognizing dual depression and addiction in the workplace can be a challenge for even the most astute managers. Fatalistic language and unusual behavior can signal a problem. An employee who confides that he or she can't go on anymore, that life has become hopeless, or that nothing is worthwhile may be struggling with undiagnosed depression. Chances are, the employee doesn't consciously recognize that depression is the cause. Behavior changes also raise a warning sign. When an employee seems to act much differently than normal, withdraw from the rest of the staff, or refuse to talk about the internal turmoil of emotions, depression may be present.

The reluctance to discuss depression in the workplace needs to be replaced by a spirit of openness and acceptance. The best place to start is through employee education. The company EAP or human resource director can make a big difference by including basic information about depression in company wellness programs, training materials, and employee communications. Access to that information can help employees suffering from depression identify symptoms in themselves and seek help. It also can help other employees recognize symptoms in their co-workers, family members, or friends. Because depressed employees can't always see the problem themselves, other employees need to be their eyes and ears. A well-informed workforce can go a long way in identifying depression and avoiding its downward slide.

INTERVENTION AND DEPRESSION

The same intervention process used to help addicted employees access treatment can be used to aid depressed employees. In both cases, early intervention can save lives. Looking the other way, or waiting for depression to correct itself, is a road map for disaster.

The interventionist chosen to facilitate should have clinical experience in treating depression. The disease is complicated and elusive and could easily throw off an inexperienced facilitator. Like substance abuse interventions, depression interventions need to be based on work-related performance and attitude issues. Hearsay won't suffice. Specificity and facts are required. Because of the connection between depression and suicide, the intervened employee should not be allowed to be alone after the intervention, even for a few minutes. Assuming that an independent managed care assessment isn't required, he or she should be moved immediately into treatment. Once admitted, he or she will be assessed by the clinical staff. The clinic or hospital needs to be lined up in advance and equipped to deal with depression as well as possible coexisting addictions. The rule of thumb when intervening on an employee with depression is caution.

Coke and Depression

Tony and an Army buddy started a catering company on Chicago's south side in the early 1970s after they both got out of the service. By all accounts, the business was successful. They had a great clientele and a reputation to match. But Tony's life was far from happy. He struggled with a cocaine addiction that he couldn't overcome, despite three rounds of chemical dependency treatment in five years. The longest he'd gone without a hit was forty-five days. He earnestly tried to follow the recommendations made by his treatment counselors and Twelve Step sponsors, but every attempt at sobriety was short lived. It was only a matter of time before he landed back where he started. One of his biggest struggles was with mood swings. He couldn't predict them, much less control them. Tony's partner tried to help him work through these bouts, but any attempt at cajoling, coddling, or calming made little difference. Tony was just miserable in sobriety.

A month after Tony's third attempt at treatment, he felt so dejected that he tried to take his own life. His partner found him slumped over the steering wheel of his car, the motor running and the garage door closed. He rushed Tony to the emergency room, where the medical staff brought him back to consciousness. In the days that followed, Tony talked about his feelings of overwhelming sadness, and at the futility of chasing sobriety. He said that he felt trapped in a body that was incapable of appreciating the positive things in life. The way he looked at it, either the coke would kill him or sobriety would. He couldn't see any other options.

The hospital where Tony was treated for asphyxiation ran some psychological tests for depression. The staff psychiatrist determined that Tony suffered from both chemical dependency and clinical depression. His depression had gone undiagnosed because his addiction veiled the symptoms. It's a tragic, but common, oversight. Cocaine use temporarily relieved his symptoms of depression, and his undiagnosed depression sabotaged the quality of sobriety. The pain of untreated depression became so intense that he eventually gave up.

Could Tony's suicide attempt been prevented? In all likelihood, yes. If he had been taking antidepressants and undergoing psychotherapy for his depression, sobriety could have been a welcome reprieve instead of a life sentence. Once his conditions were properly diagnosed and treated, he was able to stay sober and enjoy the natural highs in life.

Gambling
The Painful Stakes of Compulsive Gambling

Compulsive gambling, like other addictions, is misunderstood and largely overlooked in the American workplace. Contrary to popular Vegas stereotypes, most employees with gambling addictions are not middle-aged men sporting pinkie rings and gold chains who squander their fortunes at high-stake blackjack tables. They are men and women of all ages and every profession. Most problem gamblers are young—between twenty-five and thirty-four—and hold down respectable jobs. Their numbers are growing, thanks in part to the proliferation of casinos and state-run lotteries and to the popularity of high-risk gambling among teens. Teens who get hooked on gambling have a greater chance of carrying the habit into adulthood.

Gambling addiction rivals all other addictions in its level of self-deception and mood swings. It's cloaked in shame, denial, secrecy, premeditation, and suicidal tendencies. It's a disease of altered perceptions and tumultuous emotions. Gambling itself is just a symptom. The core problem stems from low self-esteem and a lack of self-worth. Compulsive gamblers come off as overconfident, energetic, and easily bored. They are big spenders. The underbelly of the addiction shows markings of extreme stress, anxiety, and depression. Employees who gamble compulsively use the entire ritual to subconsciously self-medicate. The thing that separates them from nonproblem gamblers is their defined loss of control around gambling. They are incapable of learning from past experience to moderate present behavior. The prospect of dire consequences does not dissuade them from throwing the dice, plugging the machine, or betting the farm. Calculated risk is a foreign concept.

The American Psychiatric Association defines pathological gambling as "the chronic and progressive failures to resist the impulses to gamble and act out gambling behavior that compromises, disrupts, or damages personal, family, or vocational pursuits."[6] This preoccupation with gambling escalates during times of stress—even when gambling itself is the cause of stress. The more trouble that gambling causes, the more the employee is compelled to gamble. It's a catch-22. Classic outcomes include severe indebtedness, default of debts and other financial obligations, disrupted family and work relationships, inattention to work, and illegal activities that are motivated by the need for money.

Employees who suffer from gambling disorders believe that money causes all their problems and that greenbacks can solve them. As their gambling escalates, they often resort to lying to get the financial resources needed to support their habit. They make no serious attempt to budget or save money. When lying fails to produce results, they turn to antisocial behavior—stealing, prostitution, or extortion—to get funds. Their friends, family, and co-workers are frequently lured into the web. Their employers become unwitting "financiers."

The Ten Symptoms of Gambling Addiction
1. Feeling guilty or being dishonest about time or money spent on gambling and its negative consequences
2. Repeated failed attempts to cut back on gambling

3. Inability to follow through with promises to self or others
4. Diversion of time and money from other obligations
5. Inordinate amounts of time thinking or fantasizing about gambling
6. Psychological or physical rush when contemplating gambling or actually doing it, followed by an emotional crash when the experience ends
7. Defending the right to gamble, no matter what
8. Using gambling as an antidote when feeling upset, anxious, depressed, or out of sorts
9. Engaging in high-risk or illegal activities to get money or possessions that can be converted to money to support the habit
10. Associating with "lower companions" to normalize high-risk gambling behaviors

BETTING ON INTERVENTION

The progressive nature of the gambling addiction eventually inspires someone in the employee's life to intercede on his or her behalf. It may be a spouse, colleague, friend, or supervisor. This is a risky and courageous move. It involves breaking the conspiracy of silence that insulates the gambler from the realities of his or her disease. If no one steps forward, the addiction continues its downward spiral, until bill collectors, bankruptcy court, or the law picks up the remnants of what had been a productive life.

In selecting an interventionist and a treatment program, it's important to choose resources that specialize in compulsive gambling. This advice holds true even if gambling is diagnosed as a secondary addiction. For intervention to be successful, the interventionist needs to understand the underpinnings of the disease. For treatment to work, gamblers need to be around other people who share their common past. They will make better progress if they can relate to their peers in treatment.

Shake, Rattle, and Roll

Leeann was the purchasing clerk for a large entertainment company based on the West Coast. Unbeknownst to her employer, she had started using company funds to support her gambling addiction, promising herself that she would pay back the money when she hit the jackpot. Accessing money was no problem. She had the authority to create purchase orders and charge items to the company credit card, against which she took cash advances.

Gambling was her little secret until one of the corporate accountants noticed a number of cash advances for the same amount of money, at the same location, over an extended period of time. The establishment was a large gambling casino located on the fringe of the city. Many of the advances were made during off-hours or on weekends. The accountant notified her department head, who took the matter to the director of human resources. After carefully monitoring Leeann's cash management activity, she confirmed that Leeann showed the signs of a gambling problem. She found no indication of chemical dependency, a common accompaniment to excessive gambling.

The HR director asked an addiction counselor and interventionist to review the case and make a recommendation. His first question was about the company's intentions. The HR director explained that the company had two objectives. The first was to get Leeann help, if possible. It valued her as an employee and wanted to retain her. The second was to put an end to the cash drain on the company and recover lost funds. It was not looking to punish Leeann. The interventionist recommended a corporate intervention.

The company assembled an intervention team that included the HR director, finance director, and in-house attorney. It deliberately kept the team small because of the sensitive nature of the problem. In the preplanning meeting, the team agreed that Leeann would need to undergo intensive inpatient gambling treatment and pay back every dollar of the misused funds. Assuming she met these requirements, the company would not file criminal charges against her. It held off on any decision regarding her job status until after she completed treatment.

At first, Leeann denied having any kind of gambling problem. When confronted with the facts, which had been assembled by the accountants, she acknowledged that she had started visiting the casino a year before, following a bitter divorce. It was an easy way to forget her troubles, she said. She started innocently enough, going once a week and spending a small amount of money each time. Without realizing it, she was making a gambling run several times a week and dropping large sums of money. When she won, she felt great. She convinced herself that the more she played the tables, the more she would win. It only took a few months for her gambling to get out of control. No matter how hard she tried, she could not stay away. When she couldn't handle the losses, she started taking advances on the company credit card, telling herself that she would reimburse the company with her winnings. They never materialized, so she kept on borrowing to win her way out of debt.

Admitting that she had stolen from her employer was the hardest thing she had ever done. Until she started gambling, Leeann said that she had never stolen anything in her life. She prided herself on principles of honesty and integrity. This conflict between what she believed and how she behaved was tearing her apart. She said she couldn't keep lying to herself and living a life of compromise and deceit.

Given Leeann's distressed state, the company decided that it would be best if she did not return to her job after treatment. She needed a fresh start. She accepted the decision without question, saying she was grateful that the company intervened and got her help. Although she lost her job, she felt as though she gained a new lease on life. She would soon be free from the bondage of her addiction.

Lifestyle Interventions

DESTRUCTIVE WORKPLACE BEHAVIORS

Every so often, it's necessary to intervene an employee whose life is out of control for reasons other than addiction. This is what I call a "lifestyle intervention." It's used when people act out behaviors that are not addictive but are destructive to themselves or others. Examples include office affairs, threatening or violent outbursts, habitual theft, and sexual harassment. Lifestyle interventions are not used for single incidents but for recurring or chronic behavior problems. They seek to interrupt patterns of destructive behavior that negatively affect the workplace.

Office Soap Opera

Hector, a medical researcher at a Houston pharmaceutical manufacturer, was having an affair with an unmarried executive secretary in the patent office. Hector assumed that no one at work knew of the liaison. In truth, everyone from the college intern to the retired CEO had heard the gossip. At first, the company dismissed the affair as a private issue between adults. The longer it progressed, however, the more problematic it became. Staff in both departments were put in the compromising position of covering for Hector when his wife called or stopped by the office. The situation was negatively affecting productivity and morale.

When Hector's wife and two college-aged children learned of the illicit affair, they stormed into the office, creating a scene and blaming the company for harboring secrets. The HR director called in a crisis interventionist to help resolve the issue and get things back to normal. The two of them scheduled an off-site meeting with Hector's colleagues and his wife. They talked about how the affair was creating pain and confusion at home and in the office. His wife said that she wanted to save the marriage but could not go on living in the shadows of the affair. His colleagues acknowledged that Hector's dishonesty had undermined his credibility and created a great deal of tension in the office. They said that if the situation weren't resolved quickly, key employees would bail.

It was obvious that something would have to give—Hector's relationship, his job, or his marriage. Status quo was no longer acceptable. The group formulated a plan for the intervention, which required Hector to end the affair and offered marriage counseling for his wife and him. She was clear that if her husband of twenty-seven years did not agree to participate, she would file for a divorce. After a second off-site planning session where everyone agreed upon his or her role, the team scheduled the intervention.

Although surprised by the meeting, Hector accepted the plan without hesitation. He confessed to being relieved at some level that the affair was out in the open, saying how difficult it was to live a double life. Despite evidence to the contrary, he said he loved his wife and family and did not want to lose them. His colleagues were very supportive. They committed themselves to helping him achieve closure in a way that avoided making anyone the victim.

The story didn't end happily ever after, but the fallout was minimal. Hector's family stayed intact, and his woman friend transferred to a medical supply company in the same city. Hector is slowly rebuilding his credibility at the firm, and the company is out of the soap opera business.

Sexual Addiction

OUT OF THE CLOSET AND INTO THE NEWS

Until recently, sexual compulsivity went unrecognized by employers, health care providers, and the public at large. It had the same invisible standing that alcoholism did in the first half of the last century. Today, this hidden addiction has captured the attention of the entire country, due to the high-profile sexual exploits of celebrities, professional athletes, and politicians. While most people still do not understand the extreme emotional pain, health risks, and shame associated with sexually addictive behavior, they are beginning to view it as an addictive disorder, not a lapse of judgment or lack of scruples. Like other clinical addictions, it is treatable if properly diagnosed.

Employees with sexual addictions share a number of traits with employees who suffer from other addictions. The most common is an attitude of denial. They go to great lengths to cover up, defend, or deny their compulsivity. Loss of control is a close second to denial. It dominates their behavior, regardless of the negative consequences that follow. At a deep emotional level, the afflicted employee simply is unable to self-regulate or manage his or her behavior. This lack of control creates a feeling of total powerlessness, another commonality of addiction. It leads to dramatic mood swings and painful isolation. Finally, sexual addiction is considered a "family illness" because it affects an entire family, system, or organization. Dysfunction flows in the wake of the disease.

While all addictions carry some degree of shame, sexual addiction is grounded in overwhelming shame. Different than guilt, which is remorse over doing bad things, shame is remorse over being a bad person. It's the great destroyer of self-worth. Sexual addiction has been called a shame-based disease because its addicts are so uncomfortable with their sexual dependency. The sexually addicted employee experiences inner conflict with both society's moral codes and his or her belief system regarding "normal sexual behaviors."

Sexual addiction often coexists with other addictive disorders such as drug addiction, alcoholism, or eating disorders. More than a third of those with sexual addictions were also chemically dependent.[7] This crossover makes the addictions tricky to accurately diagnose and treat, especially in the workplace. Multiple addictions must be treated simultaneously. If one goes untreated, it sabotages the other, setting up the employee for relapse and failure.

INTERVENING SEXUALLY ADDICTED EMPLOYEES

Because of its non-shaming approach, the process of intervention can be highly effective in helping the sexually addicted employee get help. To determine if intervention is appropriate and feasible, the interventionist and the employee who initiated the call for help gather basic profile information on the addicted employee. This fact-finding mission lays the groundwork for an initial intervention screening process, outlined in the sidebar on the next page.

Intervention Screening Process

1. *Identified patient profile.* The profile considers past consequences, pending legal action, prior treatments, family knowledge and involvement, physical health issues, psychological overview, and more.
2. *Screening.* Potential intervention team members are identified and selected.
3. *Disclosure.* The interventionist considers how much is disclosed at this stage and what happens if the employee's spouse or partner is not aware of the acting out.
4. *Logistics.* The best time and location for the intervention are discussed.
5. *Coverage.* The treatment provider, insurance, and general financial information are reviewed.
6. *Schedule.* The interventionist sets a schedule for the pre-intervention meeting.

The sensitive nature of sexual addiction in the workplace calls for special accommodations in the intervention process. For starters, intervention team members need to understand that sexual addiction is an illness. They need clear boundaries within which to frame their concerns, lest the intervention turn into a witch hunt. The employee is not on trial, even though he or she may acknowledge a tremendous level of shame. The team needs to guard against adding to this emotional burden. It only creates obstacles to treatment and recovery. Boundaries also safeguard the emotional and physical well being of team members, who often have been victimized by the employee's objectionable actions.

More than ever, the interventionist needs to be able to keep everyone focused on the primary objective of getting the employee to recognize his or her illness and get help. The interventionist encourages team members to carefully script their remarks to avoid inflammatory or accusatory language. The facts speak for themselves. The members generally write their comments on a worksheet or in a letter. After the meeting, the interventionist forwards this information to the treatment center to use as background in preparing the initial assessment. While the behavior at issue can be grounds for legal action, the interventionist is not in the business of dispensing legal advice. Instead, he or she takes a neutral, supportive stance. The interventionist does encourage all parties to protect their legal interests and rights by consulting with counsel that specializes in sexual abuse in the workplace.

Any attempt to treat sexually addicted employees needs to take into account the strong connection between shame and sexually compulsive behaviors. Success begins with a solid assessment, education, and counseling.

Checklist for a Sexual Addiction Intervention

- ❑ Identify an experienced, clinically trained interventionist.
- ❑ Clearly define perceived sexually compulsive behaviors and associated problems.
- ❑ Discuss potential intervention team members.
- ❑ Complete six-point intervention screening profile.
- ❑ Identify and discuss any pending legal issues.

- ❑ Consider conditions surrounding children, if involved.
- ❑ Discuss reporting procedures, if appropriate.
- ❑ Identify any physical health-related concerns (HIV and so on).
- ❑ Map out "Plan B" for both the afflicted employee and affected employees in case the intervention doesn't result in the employee seeking treatment. Everyone involved needs to feel safe, regardless of the outcome.

Retreat from Addiction

On the Friday before President's Day, twenty medical and administrative staff members from a specialty clinic headed to a rustic lodge in the Ozarks for a three-day, team-building retreat. On Saturday evening, the facilitator frantically approached the lodge owner for permission to use the house phone, generally reserved for emergencies. No one was hurt, he said, but he had a crisis on his hands and needed help. Collecting his wits, he placed a collect call to a colleague who specialized in sexual interventions. When the voice on the other end answered, the facilitator hastily explained what had happened during the afternoon break.

Three female staff members had asked to speak to the retreat facilitator in private. The first woman, a registered nurse, described how she had been sexually harassed and abused by the director of the clinic over the course of two years. The episodes took place in exam rooms, record rooms, and his private office. The other two women, the clinic manager and a scheduler, described similar abuses over the same period of time. They reported that there

were at least two other women on staff who also had en-
dured the doctor's unwanted advances, sexually explicit
jokes, and fondling. It wasn't until all the women got together after the morning team-building exercise that they
uncovered the shared pattern of abuse. Until then, each
had believed that she was the only victim and had suffered her humiliation in silence.

Each recounted incidents of impropriety or outright
assault. None had reported the director's actions because
they were either too embarrassed to be mixed up in something they considered scandalous, or they were too afraid
of losing their jobs. They felt isolated and victimized.
They didn't know where to turn for guidance and protection. Once they discovered that they were not alone, they
drew courage from each other and exposed the abuse.

Not sure what to make of the charges or how to help,
the facilitator listened to the women's stories and took
careful notes. After more than an hour, he stopped the
conversation, saying that he was way out of his league.
As a team builder and management consultant, he had no
experience in sexual harassment cases. Besides, the clinic
director was the person who hired him. He was caught in
the middle, unprepared and unqualified. He asked the
women's permission to call in a crisis interventionist who
specialized in sexual addiction.

The interventionist arrived early Sunday morning before most of the staff had gathered for breakfast. The facilitator postponed the first session of the day so the two of
them could strategize on what to do. They faced a highly
sensitive, complex situation with lots of issues. Not only
did they have to address the accusations of sexual misconduct directed at the doctor, but they had to make sure
the women in his employ were not further traumatized
by his actions or the intervention process.

The interventionist approached each woman individually to ask her to serve on the intervention team. All three accepted. While the facilitator and the rest of the staff wrapped up the retreat, each participant prepared a written record of specific incidents of sexual abuse, assault, or harassment for presentation during the intervention. During the planning meeting that followed, they compared notes on what they knew so that everyone was on the same page during the pending intervention. Here's what they discovered:

- The doctor presented himself as a great boss who was in complete denial of his addiction.
- His wife was totally unaware of his behavior.
- He had received treatment for alcoholism five years earlier and was still working a program of recovery and abstaining from alcohol.
- He was in good physical health and prided himself on his commitment to a daily exercise routine.
- To their knowledge, there were no legal charges pending from any of his behaviors.
- The women involved had developed a collective foundation of emotional support that enabled them to act on the sexual violations. Independently, they had been unwilling or unable to step forward. Not all of the women who had been violated were comfortable participating in the intervention process. Some were afraid of possible retribution.

Immediate action was necessary due to the seriousness of the infractions and the impact on staff and their families. The interventionist defined three objectives: (1) to interrupt the painful pattern of abuse, (2) to attempt to get the doctor appropriate help, and (3) to empower the women to take care of themselves in the most appropriate way possible. They called the intervention after lunch. It was very straightforward. Each woman read her comments and talked about how the doctor's actions had affected her life. The doctor feigned indignation at first, but shifted to resignation and remorse as the meeting progressed. He agreed to be admitted into a month-long sexual addiction program at the conclusion of the intervention. Before escorting the doctor to treatment, the interventionist advised the women to seek counseling or a support group for victims of sexual abuse when they returned home. He even recommended several therapists who specialized in this area. He also told them to take whatever legal steps they needed to take care of themselves.

Although treatment enabled the doctor to understand his actions within the context of an addiction, it in no way negated his responsibility. He remained accountable for everything he had done and faced serious consequences. Among other things, he was reported to the state Medical Licensing Board. His license to practice medicine was suspended. He also was forced to resign his position as clinic director and faced lawsuits by two members of his staff.

Computer Addiction

Hooked on the Net

Computer addiction in the workplace is a relatively new phenomenon. It first reared its head in the early 1990s, when employees gained access to computer technology on their desktops. Today, it deals mostly with their compulsion to check out of real life and log onto cyber life. A 1999 study of 18,000 Internet users classified 6 percent of the on-line population as "addicted."[8] If the projections are accurate, this number will pick up speed as the World

Wide Web gains universal adoption. Like crack, which is easy to use and quickly absorbed, the Web will become more seductive as user-friendly interfaces and ultrafast modems make it more readily available.

Computers themselves are not the problem. They are one of the most positive technological advances of the last century, making businesses phenomenally more productive and closing the information gap between people of all backgrounds, education levels, and income group. They are the great equalizer between races, industries, and countries. But like every lauded advancement, they have a dark side. Employees can use them to enhance their lives or complicate them. When computer use takes precedence over other priorities in work or personal life, it becomes an electronic wrecker with surprisingly damaging powers.

Computer addiction can include components of sexual compulsivity, cyber sex, on-line gambling, misuse of time or workaholism, avoidance disorders, shopping compulsivity, and overspending on the latest computer toys. It's the ultimate crossover addiction. Like other addictions, computer addiction can't be categorized as either a work or home problem. It bounces back and forth. At home, it pits family members against the computer in a race for the employee's love, time, and attention. The idea of competing with a machine is demoralizing enough. When the computer is used to cultivate virtual romantic relationships, it packs all the wallop of a real-life affair. At work, business priorities vie with personal interests for the employee's energy and attention. Time that should be spent on job responsibilities gets diverted to less productive and sometimes inappropriate activities. Surfing the net, even under the guise of market research, can burn up hours. Sending and responding to e-mail can become a bigger time hog than going to meetings. Chat lines, games, and other entertainment alternatives easily creep into work hours.

Computer addiction starts with an overattachment to or obsession with the computer that adversely affects other dimensions of life. It mirrors the traits of other addictions—namely loss of control, denial, powerlessness, inability to set healthy boundaries, and compulsivity. It impacts organizations by fostering dynamics of codependency, isolation, and manipulation. The computer can be used by any employee—even one with iniquitous intentions. Fraud is harder to catch and faulty products are easier to peddle because the person behind the offer is faceless. Users can adopt new identities on a whim, and people who are normally shy become bold. Married people revert to being single. Clerks pretend to be presidents—all with complete anonymity.

Employees with addictive personalities or obsessive-compulsive disorders are especially vulnerable to computer addiction. It's the latest lure, the drug of choice, for the workforce at the millennium. It can satisfy employees' need for control, their desire to escape the realities of life, their workaholic tendencies, or their fantasies. Employees can become addicted to these feelings without even knowing it. Unconscious dependency can herald a problem. So can a number of other symptoms listed in the sidebar "Ten Symptoms of Computer Addiction." A word of caution: Just because an employee spends a significant amount of time in front of his or her computer does not indicate an addiction. Likewise, employees who have other addictions do not necessarily gravitate toward the cyber addiction. The ten symptoms distinguish normal users from abusers.

Ten Symptoms of Computer Addiction

1. *Lack of control.* A demonstrated lack of control when trying to stop or limit the amount of time spent on the computer. This includes breaking promises to one's self or others, or promising to quit or cut down and not being able to do so.

2. *Covering up.* Being dishonest about or minimizing the time spent on the computer, or covering up activities on the computer.

3. *Negative consequences.* Negative consequences experienced by the computer user, friends, or family members as a direct result of time or activities on the computer.

4. *Compromising behaviors.* Participation in high-risk or normally unacceptable behaviors when using the computer, or compromising morals and values to remain anonymous and protected. The litmus test is whether a spouse, parent, or employer would approve of the activities.

5. *Dependency.* An overdeveloped reliance on the computer. The user defends his or her right to use the computer as much as desired, even if that use makes important people in his or her life feel left out or neglected. The user denies the problem and can't comprehend what other people say about his or her computer behavior.

6. *Emotional upheaval.* Mixed feelings of euphoria (a "rush") and guilt brought on by either the inordinate amount of time spent on the

computer or the abnormal behavior acted out while using the computer.

7. *Depression.* Depression or anxiety when something or someone shortens the computer time or interrupts plans to use the computer.

8. *Obsession.* Preoccupation with the computer or computer activities when not using the computer. This includes thinking about a favorite game or program while in a staff meeting or trying to meet a project deadline.

9. *Escape.* Seeking solace in the computer when feeling uncomfortable, irritated, or sad. It can be used to hide out or self-medicate when feeling uncomfortable in a relationship, avoiding tough issues, or ignoring emotions.

10. *Financial trouble.* Financial concerns or problems caused by spending money on computer hardware or software, games, on-line charges, or any other associated costs. This also includes lost income opportunities due to distraction.

TREATING COMPUTER ADDICTION

One knee-jerk solution to cyber addiction is pulling the plug on computer use for employees who can't regulate their own use. In fact, some companies strictly prohibit Web access during work hours, except for employees who have a demonstrated need. This approach handicaps their workforce by denying them the same access to market and competitive data as their competition. In a technology-driven economy where information is king, that's counterproductive. The truth is that most office employees can't function in the technology age without a modem and a mouse. Just as employees with eating addictions still need food, so employees with computer addictions still need on-line access. The answer lies in setting limits. That's part of what happens in treatment. The computer addict begins by meeting with a psychotherapist who understands this information-age addiction and can provide a new perspective on appropriate computer use. At home, the entire family is brought together as the "coaching staff." Their job is to help the addict abstain from his or her obsession through encouragement, support, and accountability. At work, co-workers and supervisors play a similar guidance role.

8

Workplace Violence

Workplace violence, like workplace addiction, is growing at an alarming rate. Reported incidents jumped by one-third between 1988 and 1994.[1] The actual increase is probably much higher, since as many as half of the incidents go unreported, according to the FBI. Employees cover up the incidents out of embarrassment or fear of repercussions. The prevalence of workplace violence should come as no surprise, since violence on the whole is on the rise, and the business world is a microcosm of American society. There's another reason as well. As chemical addiction in the workplace escalates, violence follows suit. The two maladies are closely linked. Alcohol and drugs fuel the fires of incivility, aggression, and violence. Mind-altering chemicals break down inhibitions and impair judgment, leading employees to take out their frustrations in ways that can jeopardize the safety of a department or an entire organization. Of the one million reports of on-the-job violence each year,[2] nearly a quarter involve chemicals.

Upset employees are two or three times more likely to behave violently if they use drugs or alcohol. When their temper erupts, it can be directed at other employees, customers, vendors, or innocent bystanders. In a quarter of those incidents, violence ends in suicide.[3] An untreated, addicted employee who is full of rage and resentment toward his or her employer is like an agitated soda bottle waiting to explode. The slightest pressure can blow the cap. When he or she loads up on chemicals, a powerful "disinhibitory factor" kicks in. It disconnects the employee's actions from the consequences, impairing his or her self-control and judgment. When employees act on their unchecked anger, violence often results. When they sober up, rationality returns. Unfortunately, it's often too late. They can't undo the havoc they created while under the influence or restore the lives they destroyed. Rage and chemicals can be a deadly combination.

Despite media portrayals to the contrary, random shootings and bombings are still relatively rare on the American work front. Most on-the-job violence involves robbery, assault, harassment, and destruction of company property—often by employees or former employees. Many of these incidents are linked to alcohol and drugs. The toll in human and financial terms is enormous. In 1995, the Workplace Violence Research Institute put the tab at $35 billion—including litigation, lost productivity, and damage control.[4] The number swells every year.

Violence in the Extreme

Workplace violence covers the gambit from verbal threats to murder. The Bureau of Labor Statistics puts the number of work-related killings at more than 1,000 per year.[5] Many of the homicides are linked to robbery. Others, like the sensational drive-by shootings that headline the evening news, are triggered by anger and frustration gone astray. Sadly, anger is becoming more widespread in the American workforce. Nearly half of the employees polled by Gallop in 1999 described themselves as at least a little angry at work. That's up from a fourth in 1996.[6] Those who are disgruntled after being terminated, fired, or laid off pose the gravest danger. They are the faces behind a significant number of rampage attacks in the workplace.

Homicide is the leading cause of occupational death for female workers in the United States. It ranks third for male workers.[7] The fact that men outnumber women in the workforce by a slight margin accounts for only part of the disparity. The main reason is that women employees are still considered easier targets for assault than their male counterparts. The numbers are more disturbing when race figures into the equation. Statisticians count twice as many work-related murders among employees of color.[8] This sad anomaly can't be explained away by actuarial averages. The negative effects of racism, oppression, and depressed economic standing contribute greatly.

Understanding Workplace Violence

Although the relationship between chemical use and workplace violence is well established, other triggers of on-the-job violence are frequently contested. High stress levels, life balance issues, job insecurity fueled by downsizing and takeovers, and isolation are frequently cited. The bombardment of violent messages and images from the media and marketers also is blamed. Hollywood and Madison Avenue normalize violence by presenting it as an acceptable way to deal with anger and resentment. Children especially are vulnerable to media brutality, but adults are impressionable as well. A steady diet of violence can spark errant behavior in even the most acquiescent employees. Those plagued by personal problems are more susceptible to outbursts. Since employees don't have an emotional on/off switch, home issues naturally carry over to the workplace. That's why employee assistance programs are so valuable. They deal with anything that interferes with the employee's ability to do his or her job, whether it's personal or work-related. They can help employees work through frustrations before they hit the crisis mark.

Ten Traits of Violence-Prone Employees[9]
1. Have difficulty with authority figures
2. Have problems with drugs or alcohol
3. Have a history of mental health problems
4. Have a history of violence outside of work
5. Are loners and isolated at work
6. Are white men over the age of thirty-five
7. Have a bad attitude or history of violence toward women
8. Are fascinated by the military, guns, or weapons
9. Hold a grudge and seem angry most of the time
10. Are extremists

Workers' response to on-the-job violence is mixed. More than half of the employees who experience workplace incivility contemplate changing jobs. More than a fourth lose work time trying to avoid the person with whom they're in conflict. Many intentionally decrease the quality of their work.[10] Managers have an equally hard time. Most experience a half dozen aggressive acts by employees each year—generally in response to negative feedback on performance. The issue is cause for concern at all levels. The likelihood of being involved in an act of aggression while at work is real. Anyone can be a victim. This knowledge makes employees and customers skittish. It undermines basic trust, and narrows personal and professional boundaries. Rules of workplace behavior are recast as employees become more guarded. They look to their employers for protection and reassurance. The law requires that employers provide it.

The Legal Side of Workplace Violence

The Occupational Safety and Health Administration (OSHA) passed the Compliance Assistance Authorization Act in 1970 and last amended it in 1998. The act requires companies to provide safe and healthful working conditions for their employees.[11] This includes safeguarding the workplace against foreseeable harm. Companies can begin to meet this obligation by having and enforcing a Workforce Violence Prevention Plan, covered later in this chapter. At its core, the plan helps employers detect and avoid foreseeable acts of violence and aggression.

The best reason for instituting a Workplace Violence Prevention Plan is that all employees have the right to feel safe from harm while at work. Beyond that, there are many practical reasons to put a plan in place. It helps keep minor incidents in check, so they don't explode into major ones. This minimizes the risk of serious harm to potential victims. Since violence negatively affects witnesses as well as targeted victims, any plan that reduces the chance of workplace violence helps the entire organization. Violence breeds fear. Fear distracts employees, lowers morale, erodes productivity, increases absenteeism, and causes higher turnover. Finally, workplace violence, like a tornado, hits when the organization is least prepared to handle it. Having a plan in place puts organizations in a proactive, rather than reactive, mode.

Companies can face serious legal and financial exposure when violence strikes. In extreme cases, legal claims can cost millions. Liability expert Norman Bates has tracked the size of legal settlements against employers since the early 1980s. For cases that settled out of court, the average award was $500,000. For those that went to trial, the number leaped to $3 million.[12] Most claims are made on the basis of "wrongful action" or "inaction." Wrongful action centers on negligent hiring or retention of high-risk employees. If an employer has knowledge of a potentially harmful situation and does not respond to it, the company can be held liable if someone gets hurt. Take the case of a nightclub that knowingly hires a bouncer who has been fired from other clubs for physically harassing female employees. If the bouncer assaults one of the nightclub's employees, the establishment could be considered negligent for putting its employees in harm's way. "Inaction" occurs when the company fails to take reasonable action in protecting its employees. An example is neglecting to do routine background and reference checks on new hires.

The Impostor

A female employee of a major retail chain was raped and beaten by a co-worker who had been hired six months earlier. The woman sued her employer for negligence, contending that the retailer failed to verify the man's application for employment. Had it done so, the company would have discovered that the man was an ex-convict with a record of criminal sexual assault and armed robbery. His resumé said that he had spent the previous four years in college. In fact, he had been doing time in federal prison. He was out on parole when he applied for the job and made up most of the information on the application. He was a dangerous impostor who passed as a promising new hire.

The court awarded the victim $1 million in damages based on the company's negligent hiring practices. A routine background check could have avoided the tragedy and saved the retailer a bundle in damages, legal fees, and lost time. It was an expensive reminder of the necessity to follow hiring policies that include thorough background checks.

Developing a Workplace Violence Prevention Plan

The single most important step an organization can make in preventing on-the-job violence and aggression is developing a Workplace Violence Prevention Plan. There are many different approaches. The best starting point is the handbook, "Dealing with Workplace Violence: A Guide for Agency Planners."[13] Published by the U.S. Office of Personnel Management—the equivalent of the federal government's HR department—it's the bible on violence prevention for both public and private sector organizations. The handbook is available in print or on-line (*www.opm.gov/workplac/index.html-ssi*). It outlines four basic planning steps:

1. *Assess the organization's current ability to handle potentially violent situations.* Start by reviewing past incidents and evaluating how effectively they were handled. Look for patterns, like a particular work group or plant that has a higher share of affrontive incidents. Then take an inventory of staff skills and expertise that could prove useful in resolving potentially explosive situations. These skills might include mediation, conflict resolution, crisis counseling, or investigative work. Finally, examine the security procedures and systems already in place to ensure that they are adequate.

2. *Fill in the skill gaps.* Even large organizations have skill deficiencies. Figure out what they are, and either train existing staff to fill the need or go outside the organization. Tap local resources such as police, mental health providers, university experts, and so on. Don't wait until the crisis hits to start assembling the list.

3. *Design a reporting procedure for employees.* The goal is to encourage employees to report all incidents, even small ones. The reporting process can be handled through a hot line, direct reports to supervisors, or a number of other means. The approach is less important than the way in which reports are handled— quickly, confidentially, and effectively. Word spreads quickly when a report is made and nothing is done to resolve it, or the process gets botched. Success hinges on building credibility among employees. Before launching a reporting procedure, make sure that the staff fielding the reports are well trained and responsive. It's also critical that they have the backing of senior management.

4. *Develop plans to respond to violent incidents.* Given the wide range of behaviors that constitute workplace violence, it's useful to categorize incidents before deciding on a course of action. Categories could be based on urgency (emergency or nonemergency), type of behavior (threats, bullying, disruptions, physical assault, or suicide), or type of aggressor (employee, customer, or outsider). Whatever action is recommended for each category, the person or office charged with implementation must be given broad latitude to resolve the issue in the best way possible. Every situation is different. Flexibility is a must.

Tips for Effective Violence Prevention Plans

- *Take every threat seriously.* Employees will not share their concerns if they think management will minimize or ignore them.
- *Be realistic.* Even the best plan cannot prevent all workplace violence. It's too unpredictable. However, businesses can reduce their risk of violence by being proactive and responding swiftly to the first signs of threats, intimidation, harassment, and other inappropriate behaviors.
- *Get buy-in from the top.* All members of management must publicly back the plan for it to have muscle. The plan is only as good as the organization's ability to implement and enforce it.
- *Avoid absolute language like "zero tolerance."* It can backfire by discouraging employees from reporting minor infractions that might appear to get a co-worker fired. It can strip the organization of the latitude it needs to deal with unanticipated situations. Absolutes also may work against a company in the courtroom.
- *Make it simple.* If employees can't understand the policy, they won't follow it.
- *Put the policy in writing.* A written policy statement on violence prevention is generally more effective in calming employee fears, encouraging reporting, and building credibility than an unwritten plan.

The written policy should make it clear that all employees are responsible for maintaining a safe work environment. It also should define the scope of protection—not just physical violence, but harassment, intimidation, and other disruptive behaviors committed by people inside and outside the organization. Employees need to be reassured that the company will respond to all reports and will attempt to stop any behavior that threatens, frightens, or harms them. The Workplace Violence Research Institute in Palm Springs, California, published a workplace violence prevention program in 1998 that provides a simple model for organizations of any size to follow.[14] Like the U.S. Office of Personnel Management plan, it stresses simplicity, brevity, and clarity. (See the sidebar below.)

Creating a Workplace Violence Prevention Program

- Form a planning committee—including representatives of management, the union, general counsel, employee relations or human resources, the EAP, and security.
- Assess current conditions.
- Fix and implement policies.
- Establish a confidential information and assessment hot line.
- Develop a training program.
- Review and improve pre-employment screening practices.
- Review and refine the termination and lay-off process.
- Prepare a crisis response plan.
- Test and improve the program on a continuing basis.

Domestic Violence at the Workplace

Domestic violence and workplace violence are two sides of the same coin. Where one exists, the other follows. That's the reason that domestic violence continues to top the list of corporate security concerns. Conflicts that begin at home are often finished at work. The enraged person knows where to find his or her spouse or partner and tracks down the employee in the parking lot, the lunchroom, or cubical. Co-workers become unwitting witnesses to domestic aggression in the workplace. This has a devastating effect on the staff. On a psychological level, it plants the seeds of fear, distrust, and anxiety. On a business level, it destroys productivity. Like family members who refuse to recognize violent behavior for what it is, some companies turn their backs on violence in their midst. The mindset of "it will never happen to us" is called "institutional denial." Despite warnings and better judgment, the attitude often prevails until something tragic happens to jar the company back to reality.

Too Little, Too Late

A receptionist at a Long Island bank punched into work at 8:30 A.M. and was lying in a pool of blood by 9 A.M. Her estranged boyfriend had followed her into work and shot her in the head while she fielded a customer call about on-line banking. Her parents sued the company for negligent security. Their claim was based on the fact that their daughter had told her employer that a restraining order had been issued against her boyfriend after he tried to run her over in his car. She told the branch manager that she feared for her life and asked to be temporarily relocated to a less exposed workstation. He agreed to look into the matter but didn't take her concern seriously. She was dead a week later.

The suit was settled in 1995 for a half million dollars. This case drives home two points. It illustrates how a problem that starts at home can follow an employee to work. It also underlines the importance of responding to employees' safety needs with due haste.

Violence Intervention

Intervention can be used to interrupt most any pattern of disruptive behavior that threatens the workplace. It works with raging employees who are sober, as well as those whose violent tendencies are exacerbated by drugs or alcohol. Intervention is designed to forestall crisis, however it reveals itself in the workplace. It's a powerful weapon in an organization's arsenal of defense against violence.

The trick to an effective violence intervention is identifying the problem before it erupts. Warning signs of pending violence can be difficult to identify because so much of violence is impulsive and unplanned. However, careful observers can often spot disenchanted employees who are potentially dangerous. The employees' discontent clings to them like a long shadow at the end of the day. Other employees can't help but cross the path of their misery. If the company has a process in place for flagging troublesome behavior, and employees feel comfortable using it, they can help avert a precarious situation. Concerned employees also can work through the employee assistance program. It's there to help them resolve problematic issues.

EAPs play an important role in the corporate crusade to reduce workplace violence. A majority of employees feel comfortable bringing personal problems to their EAP. In contrast, a full two-thirds would not share those issues with their HR department.[15] EAPs are conduits of sensitive information and solutions. Employees trust them and depend on them for advice and direction. They need to be integrated into any effective Workplace Violence Prevention Program.

Checklist on Violence Prevention Preparedness

1. Is a written policy in place that clearly outlines requirements and procedures for handling reports of workplace violence?
2. Has the company communicated the policies and procedures to employees? Are written materials available that describe the program?
3. Is the person charged with administering the program given the authority to manage it?
4. Has the organization made sufficient attempts to learn about employees or candidates who have a history of illegal behavior? Has it acted responsibly in delegating authority to such persons?
5. Has the organization developed an internal program to monitor its compliance standards?
6. Does the company have a process that protects employees who report criminal conduct in the workplace?
7. Does the company consistently enforce its disciplinary actions?
8. Does the organization have a process for guarding against repeat incidents?

Random Acts

On its fifth anniversary in business, a building materials manufacturer formed a task force to design a company wellness program. Ted, a first-line supervisor with a history of heavy off-the-job drinking, volunteered to serve on the planning team in hope of restoring some balance to his life. Things at home were in turmoil. His wife had threatened to leave him. His two teenage children were acting out and had become unmanageable. His job wasn't going much better. Production quotas were way off, and quality had taken a plunge. He couldn't seem to motivate his crew and got no help from management. He was restless, unhappy, and frustrated. He confided in friends that his world was falling apart. They urged him to talk to the EAP, but he was afraid that the company might point to his drinking as part of the problem. He told himself that as long as he didn't drink at work, his drinking was under control. He kept his troubles to himself and plodded ahead.

During the three-month wellness project, Ted's drinking escalated. Word in the plant was that he never dried out between one evening blitz and the next. Although his crew worried about him, they didn't take any action. Neither did his boss, who wrote off his irritable state as trouble on the home front. At many levels, denial was at work.

One evening, the company's human resources director called the president in a panic. Ted had been arrested after a shooting rampage at the plant. It was after the second shift, so no one was hurt. Neighbors heard the shots and called the police. They apprehended Ted, hunting rifle in one hand and whiskey bottle in the other. He was handcuffed and put in jail.

The HR director called in a crisis counselor to help

them work through the fallout. They hired a public relations firm to handle the media while they focused on the staff. The interventionist held a series of confidential meetings with employees who were close to Ted. The goal was to find out what prompted the assault and how it could have been avoided. People were candid about their observations. Most knew that Ted had a drinking problem and that it was getting out of control. They also acknowledged their reluctance to act. Some felt uncomfortable with confrontation. Others were afraid of sparking Ted's anger. Others, including Ted's boss, didn't feel that they had the training to handle such a sensitive issue. His boss didn't ask for direction from his manager because he felt that it might make him appear less competent. Insecurity bred inaction. Because no one in the organization took a proactive stance, they all backed themselves into a tight reactive corner.

The counselor also talked with Ted, his family, and friends. He discovered that much of Ted's resentment toward the company was attributable to benign neglect. He had been crying out for help for months. He believed that either no one heard his pleas or no one cared enough to intervene. He felt alone and isolated at work and unloved at home. In desperation, he did something drastic. The shooting incident was Ted's way of making sure that everyone at work understood the intensity of his pain.

Two days later, the staff held a mandatory debriefing. They drew on information gathered in the interviews and talked about how they could have handled the situation differently. The wellness taskforce opted to put its work on hold and concentrate instead on a violence prevention plan. Employees from every division were asked to submit their ideas. The final plan was unveiled at an all-employee meeting the following month.

Conclusion

Addiction is a creeping vine that has invaded the American workplace. It's as common as ivy, as poisonous as sumac. Its thorns can discourage the most avid corporate gardeners from disturbing its tendrils. Once it takes hold, addiction can spread over an organization, choking the life out of departments and destroying what once was a thriving, productive garden. The fast-growing vine of addiction, in all its varieties, is a chore to uproot. But it can be done if organizations have the resolve to act and the tools to be effective. Intervention is first of those tools. It separates the employee from the disease, enabling both the individual and the organization to begin to heal. As any gardener knows, it's easier to make progress if you take action early, before the shoots of addiction are deep-rooted. Treatment is the second tool in the task of reclamation. It's about starting over and reclaiming lost potential. Recovery is the third. This is the life-long process of tending the garden and keeping it healthy. It's what employees in recovery do every day of their lives.

Businesses that struggle with addiction and other destroyers of human potential have reason to be hopeful. Addiction is both treatable and preventable. By understanding their role in the recovery process, and having the courage to act, they can help addicted employees become productive again, curb the financial drain on their organizations, and become healthy, thriving businesses.

Resource Guide

Advocacy and Education

American Council for Drug Education
164 West 74th Street
New York, NY 10023
(800) 488-3784
www.acde.org

Children of Alcoholics Foundation
164 West 74th Street
New York, NY 10023
(800) 359-2623
www.adultchildren.org

Community Anti-Drug Coalitions of America
901 North Pitt Street, Suite 300
Alexandria, VA 22314
(800) 542-2322
www.cadca.org

Council on Prevention Education: Substances
845 Barret Avenue
Louisville, KY 40204
(502) 583-6820
www.copes.org

Higher Education Center for Alcohol and Other Drug
Prevention
55 Chapel Street
Newton, MA 02458
(800) 676-1730
www.edc.org/hec

National Alliance for the Mentally Ill
Colonial Place Three
2107 Wilson Boulevard, Suite 300
Arlington, VA 22201
(800) 950-6264
www.nami.org

National Association for Children of Alcoholics
11426 Rockville Pike, Suite 100
Rockville, MD 20852
(888) 554-2627
www.health.org/nacoa

National Mental Health Association
1021 Prince Street
Alexandria, VA 22314
(800) 969-6642
www.nmha.org

National Organization on Fetal Alcohol Syndrome
216 G Street NE
Washington, DC 20002
(202) 785-4585
www.nofas.org

Federal Agencies

Center for Substance Abuse Prevention
5600 Fishers Lane, Rockwall II
Rockville, MD 20857
(301) 443-0365
www.samhsa.gov/csap/index.html
e-mail: nnadal@samhsa.gov

Department of Justice
Office on the Americans with Disabilities Act
Civil Rights Division
P.O. Box 66118
Washington, DC 20035-6118
(800) 514-0301
www.usdoj.gov/crt/ada/adahom1.htm

Department of Transportation
Drug Enforcement Program and Program Compliance
400 Seventh Street SW
Washington, DC 20590
(800) 225-3784

Equal Employment Opportunity Commission
1801 L Street NW
Washington, DC 20507
(202) 663-4900
www.eeoc.gov

National Clearinghouse for Alcohol and Drug Information
P.O. Box 2345
Rockville, MD 20847-2345
(800) 729-6686
www.health.org

National Institute for Occupational Safety and Health
4676 Columbia Parkway
Mail Stop C-13
Cincinnati, OH 45226
(800) 356-4674
www.cdc.gov/niosh/homepage.html
e-mail: pubstaft@cdc.gov

National Institute of Mental Health
6001 Executive Boulevard, Room 8184
MSC 9663
Bethesda, MD 20892-9663
(301) 443-4513
www.nimh.nih.gov

National Institute on Drug Abuse
6001 Executive Boulevard
Bethesda, MD 20892-9561
(301) 443-1124
www.nida.nih.gov

Substance Abuse and Mental Health Services Administration
Room 12-105 Parklawn Building
5600 Fishers Lane
Rockville, MD 20857
(301) 443-4795
www.samhsa.gov

U.S. Department of Health and Human Services
Center for Disease Control and Prevention
National Center for Health Statistics
Division of Data Services
Hyattsville, MD 20782-2003
(301) 458-4636
www.cdc.gov/nchs

U.S. Department of Labor
Office of Public Affairs
200 Constitution Avenue NW
Room S-1032
Washington, DC 20210
(202) 693-4650

U.S. Department of Labor
Occupational Safety and Health Administration
Office of Public Affairs
200 Constitution Avenue NW, Room N-3649
Washington, DC 20210
(202) 693-1999

U.S. National Library of Medicine
8600 Rockville Pike
Bethesda, MD 20894
(888) 346-3656
(301) 594-5983
www.nlm.nih.gov

Information and Help Lines

Americans with Disabilities Information Line
(800) 514-0301
TDD (800) 514-0383

Center for Substance Abuse Treatment
(800) 662-HELP

National Cocaine Help Line
(800) COCAINE

National Council on Alcoholism and
Drug Dependence Hope Line
(800) NCA-CALL

Workplace Help Line of the Center for
Substance Abuse Prevention (CSAP)
(800) WORKPLACE

Professional Associations

American Counseling Association
5999 Stevenson Avenue
Alexandria, VA 22304-3300
(800) 347-6647
www.counseling.org

American Medical Association
515 North State Street
Chicago, IL 60610
(312) 464-5000
www.ama-assn.org

American Mental Health Counselors Association
801 North Fairfax Street, Suite 304
Alexandria, VA 22314
(800) 326-2642
www.amhca.org/home

American Psychiatric Association
1400 K Street NW
Washington, DC 20005
(202) 682-6000
www.psych.org

American Psychological Association
750 First Street NE
Washington, DC 20002-4242
(202) 336-5500
www.apa.org

American Society of Addiction Medicine
4601 North Park Avenue, Suite 101, Arcade Level
Chevy Chase, MD 20815
(301) 656-3920
www.asam.org

Association of Intervention Specialists, Inc.
15200 Shady Grove Road, Suite 350
Rockville, MD 20850
(301) 296-4330

Employee Assistance Professionals Association (EAPA)
2101 Wilson Boulevard, Suite 500
Arlington, VA 22201
(703) 387-1000
www.eap-association.org

National Association of Alcoholism and
Drug Abuse Counselors
1911 North Fort Myer Drive, Suite 900
Arlington, VA 22209
(800) 548-0497
www.naadac.org

National Association of State Alcohol/Drug Abuse Directors
808 17th Street NW, Suite 410
Washington, DC 20006
(202) 293-0090
www.nasadad.org

National Council on Sexual Addiction and Compulsivity
1090 Northcase Parkway, Suite 200
South Marietta, GA 30067
(770) 989-9754
www.ncsac.org

National Nurses Society on Addictions
4101 Lake Boone Trail, Suite 201
Raleigh, NC 27607
(919) 783-5871
www.nnsa.org

Self-Help and Support Groups

Al-Anon Family Group Headquarters
1600 Corporate Landing Parkway
Virginia Beach, VA 23454-5617
(888) 425-2666

Alateen
1600 Corporate Landing Parkway
Virginia Beach, VA 23454-5617
(800) 356-9996

Alcoholics Anonymous
General Service Office
475 Riverside Drive
New York, NY 10015
(212) 870-3400

Co-Anon Family Groups
P.O. Box 12124
Tucson, AZ 85732-2124
(520) 513-5028

Cocaine Anonymous (CA)
P.O. Box 2000
Los Angeles, CA 90049-8000
(310) 559-5833

Depressed Anonymous
P.O. Box 17471
Louisville, KY 40217
(502) 569-1989

Families Anonymous, Inc.
P.O. Box 3475
Culver City, CA 90231-3475
(818) 989-7841

Gamblers Anonymous
P.O. Box 17173
Los Angeles, CA 90017
(213) 386-8789

Marijuana Anonymous
P.O. Box 2912
Van Nuys, CA 91404
(800) 766-6779

Nar-Anon Family Group Headquarters
P.O. Box 2562
Palos Verdes Peninsula, CA 90274
(310) 547-5800

Narcotics Anonymous
P.O. Box 9999
Van Nuys, CA 91409
(818) 773-9999

National Mental Health Consumers' Self-Help Clearinghouse
1211 Chestnut Street, Suite 1207
Philadelphia, PA 19107
(800) 553-4539

Nicotine Anonymous
P.O. Box 126338
Harrisburg, PA 17112-6338
(415) 750-0328

Sexaholics Anonymous
P.O. Box 111910
Nashville, TN 37222
(615) 331-6230

Chemical Guide

This chart of legal and controlled substances is adapted from *The Drug-Free Workplace,* a free pamphlet published by Business and Legal Reports.[1] To order a copy, call (800) 727-5257. All of the substances listed are addictive. All negatively impact mental and physical abilities and impair workplace performance.

Legal Substances	Other Names	Physical Risks	Workplace and Behavior Risks
Alcohol	Booze Liquor	Highly addictive	Lessens concentration and impairs judgment, causing dangerous or problematic behavior
		Loss of sleep and appetite	Lowers productivity and increases the workload on others
		Liver and kidney damage from prolonged use	Retards ability to deal with problems or stress, reducing job effectiveness
		Overdose and death	Alienates other employees
Amphetamines	Speed Uppers Meth Ice Crystal	Addictive	Pushes employee beyond normal physical ability, putting him or her and other employees at risk

Legal Substances	Other Names	Physical Risks	Workplace and Behavior Risks
Amphetamines (continued)		Brain damage	Causes accidents and injuries
		Overdose and death	Results in hyper, careless activity
Sedatives	Downers Goofball 'Ludes	Addictive	Is dangerous in jobs requiring mental alertness and equipment/machinery operation
		Slows mental processes and reflexes	Disrupts relationships
		Liver and kidney damage from prolonged use	Steals energy and motivation
		Overdose and death	
Marijuana	Pot Grass Weed	Slows physical reflexes	Throws off perceptions of space and time
		Lessens mental powers and impairs brain function	Increases incidence of accidents and injuries
		Damage to lungs and reproductive system	Causes forgetfulness

Illegal Substances	Other Names	Physical Risks	Workplace and Behavior Risks
Cocaine	Coke Snow Freebase Crack Rock	Highly addictive	Causes temporary feeling of super-human power
		Damage to respiratory and immune system	Causes emotional problems and wild mood swings
		Malnutrition	Impairs judgment and decision making
		Seizures	Makes employees less dependable
		Loss of brain function	Drives employees to steal to cover the cost
		Overdose and death	
Heroin	Junk H Horse	Highly addictive, even in small doses	Causes total disregard for workplace safety—or anything except the drug
		Physical breakdown	Drives employees to steal to pay for the drug
		Disease from dirty needles or other paraphernalia	Lowers productivity and ability to manage job
		Severe infections—including hepatitis and AIDS	Destroys relationships
		Overdose, coma, and death	

Illegal Substances	Other Names	Physical Risks	Workplace and Behavior Risks
Hallucinogens (Some new forms are not yet covered by drug laws, but eventually will be classified as illegal.)	PCP LSD Ecstasy (MDMA) Angel Dust Designer drugs	Hallucinations that distort what's seen and heard	Puts employees in danger or employees fail to recognize dangers
		Emotional disturbances	Causes sudden and bizarre changes in behavior, including attacks on others
		Flashback panic	Causes flashbacks, loss of concentration or memory, and behavior problems long after drug has worn off
		Depression	
		Mental breakdown	

Notes

Chapter 1: The Cost of Addiction

1. P. Mrazek, *Preventing Mental Health and Substance Abuse Problems in Managed Health Care Settings* (Alexandria, Va.: National Mental Health Association, Office of Managed Care, 1998).

2. U.S. Department of Health and Human Services, Substance Abuse and Mental Health Services Administration, Office of Applied Studies, *1997 National Household Survey on Drug Abuse* (Rockville, Md.: DHHS, 1998).

3. Ibid.

4. "Addiction in the Workplace Survey" (Center City, Minn.: Hazelden Foundation, 1996).

5. M. Bernstein and J. J. Mahoney, "Management Perspectives on Alcoholism: The Employers Stake in Alcoholism Treatment," *Occupational Medicine* 4, no. 2 (1989): 223–32.

6. Institute for Health Policy, Brandeis University, *Substance Abuse: The Nation's Number One Problem, Key Indicators for Policy* (Princeton, N.J.: Robert Wood Johnson Foundation, 1993), 8.

7. A. Merrill, "Drugs in the Workplace Remain a Confusing and Complex Issue," *Minneapolis Star Tribune*, 19 August 1994.

8. U.S. Department of Health and Human Services, National Institutes of Health, National Institute on Alcohol Abuse and Alcoholism, National Institute on Drug Abuse "The Economic Costs of Alcohol and Drug Abuse in the United States," (Rockville, Md.: DHHS, 1992).

9. Mrazek, *Preventing Mental Health and Substance Abuse Problems in Managed Health Care Settings.*

10. "Substance Abuse: A Silent Threat," *Health Care Trends* (Business First of Columbus, Inc., 22 March 1993).

11. Ibid.

12. Institute for Health Policy, Brandeis University, *Substance Abuse: The Nation's Number One Problem, Key Indicators for Policy,* 44.

13. T. W. Mangione, J. Howland, and M. Lee, *New Perspectives for Workplace Strategies: Results from Corporate Drinking Study* (Boston: JSI Training Institute, 1998).

14. N. S. Bell et al., "Workplace Barriers to the Effective Management of Alcohol Problems," *Journal of Occupational and Environmental Medicine* (December 1996): 1213–19.

15. CATOR/New Standards, Inc., *Cost Effectiveness System to Measure Drug and Alcohol Treatment Outcomes.* Conducted for the Ohio Department of Alcohol and Drug Addiction Services, Evaluation and Research Unit (Columbus), 1995.

Chapter 2: Recognizing Addiction

1. *Substance Abuse Prevention in the Workplace: An Employer Guide,* funded by the Robert Wood Johnson Foundation and Mutual of Omaha to accompany the Bill Moyers PBS special *Moyers on Addiction: Close to Home* (March 1998).

2. "Public Policy of ASAM: Definition of Addiction," approved by board of directors (Chevy Chase, Md.: American Society of Addiction Medicine [ASAM], 1990).

3. Ibid.

4. U.S. Department of Health and Human Services, Substance Abuse and Mental Health Services Administration, Office of Applied Studies, *An Analysis of Worker Drug Use and Workplace Policies and Programs* (Rockville, Md.: DHHS, 1997).

5. U.S. Department of Health and Human Services, Substance Abuse and Mental Health Services Administration,

Office of Applied Studies, *1993 National Household Survey on Drug Abuse* (Rockville, Md.: DHHS, 1994).

6. A. Leshner, "Science-based Views of Drug Addiction and Its Treatment," *Journal of American Medical Association (JAMA)* 282, no. 14 (October 3, 1999).

7. C. P. O'Brien, "A Range of Research-based Pharmacotherapies for Addiction," *Science* 278 (1997): 66–70.

8. *Survey of Employees Who Sought Help for Drug Abuse* (Washington, D.C.: U.S. Chamber of Commerce, 1997).

9. J. McGinnis and W. Foege, "Actual Cause of Deaths in the United States," *Journal of the American Medical Association (JAMA)* 270, no. 18 (November 10, 1993): 2208.

10. *Diagnostic and Statistical Manual of Mental Disorders*, 4th ed. (Washington, D.C.: American Psychiatric Association, 1994).

11. *How an Alcoholic Employee Behaves* (Waverly, Minn.: New Beginnings Treatment Center, 1994).

12. E. M. Jellinek, "Phases of Alcohol Addiction," *Quarterly Journal of Studies on Alcohol* 13 (1952): 673–84.

13. "20 Questions: Are You an Alcoholic?" (Baltimore, Md.: John Hopkins University Hospital).

Chapter 3: The Intervention Process

1. V. E. Johnson, *Intervention: How to Help Someone Who Doesn't Want Help* (Minneapolis, Minn.: The Johnson Institute, 1989).

2. J. Fearing, "Comparing Outcomes Between Intervened and Self-Referred Patients," *Treatment Today* 8, no. 2 (1996): 10–11.

3. Ibid.

Chapter 4: Models of Intervention

1. R. Meyers, W. R. Miller, D. Hill, and S. Tonigan, Community Reinforcement and Family Training (CRAFT),

"Engaging Unmotivated Drug Users in Treatment," *Journal of Substance Abuse* 10, no. 3 (1999): 291–308.

2. M. T. French, G. A. Zarkin, J. W. Bray, and T. D. Hartwell, *Cost of Employee Assistance Programs: Findings from a National Survey* (Research Triangle Park, N.C.: Research Triangle Institute, 1994).

3. M. Falco, *The Making of a Drug-Free America: Programs That Work* (New York: Times Books, 1994).

4. National Clearinghouse for Alcohol and Drug Information, *Alcohol, Tobacco and Other Drugs in the Workplace*. More information available on-line at www.health.org.

Chapter 5: The Treatment Process

1. U.S. Department of Health and Human Services, National Institutes of Health, National Institute on Drug Abuse, *NIDA Notes* 12, no. 8 (1997).

Chapter 6: Legal Issues of Addiction

1. T. Sheehan, "Addicted Employees Need Help, Not Pink Slips," *Minneapolis City Business* (16 February 1998).

2. Equal Employment Opportunity Commission (EEOC), *Facts about the Americans with Disabilities Act* (Washington, D.C., 1997).

3. Equal Employment Opportunity Commission (EEOC), *The Americans with Disabilities Act: A Brief Overview* (Washington, D.C., 1998).

4. *Americans with Disabilities Act of 1990*. Congress.

5. "Telephone Survey," (Center City, Minn.: Hazelden Foundation, 1999).

6. EEOC, *Facts about the Americans with Disabilities Act*.

7. *Equal Employment Opportunity Commission v. Exxon* (5th Cir. 2000).

8. United Nations World Health Organization. New York.

9. U.S. Department of Labor, "How to Establish a Workplace Substance Abuse Program," *Working Partners for an Alcohol-and Drug-Free Workplace* (Washington, D.C., 1998).

10. Sheehan, "Addicted Employees Need Help, Not Pink Slips."

11. *Drug-Free Workplace Act of 1998* (Old Saybrook, Conn.: Business and Legal Reports, Inc., 1999).

12. "Questions and Answers about the Mental Health Parity Act," *HR Magazine* (March 1997).

13. U.S. Department of Health and Human Services, *Confidentiality of Patients' Records and Other Drug Treatment,* Technical Assistance Publication (Washington, D.C., 1994).

Chapter 7: Other Addictions and Depression

1. D. A. Reiger et al., "One-Month Prevalence of Mental Disorders in the United States Based on Five Epidemiological Catchment Area Sites," *Archives of General Psychiatry* 45 (1998): 977–86. R. C. Kessler et al., "Lifetime and 12-Month Prevalence of DSM-III Psychiatric Disorders in the United States," *Archives of General Psychiatry* 51 (1994): 8–9.

2. P. Mrazek, *Preventing Mental Health and Substance Abuse Problems in Managed Health Care Settings* (Alexandria, Va.: National Mental Health Association, Office of Managed Care, 1998).

3. D. Conti and W. Burton, "The Economic Impact of Depression in the Workplace," *JOM* 36, no. 9 (September 1994): 983–98.

4. U.S. Department of Health and Human Services, National Institutes of Health, National Institute of Mental Health, "Depression Research Fact Sheet" (Rockville, Md.: DHHS, 1996).

5. "Conquering Depression," *NARSAD Research* (1996). Available at www.mhsource.com/advocacy/narsad.dep.html.

6. *Diagnostic and Statistical Manual of Mental Disorders,*

4th ed. (Washington, D.C.: American Psychiatric Association, 1994), diagnostic code 312.31.

7. P. Carnes, *Don't Call It Love: Recovery from Sexual Addiction* (New York: Bantam Doubleday Dell, 1991).

8. E. Zorn, "Cyberfuture Bound to Lure More into Web Addiction," *Chicago Tribune*, Internet edition, 13 January 2000.

Chapter 8: Workplace Violence

1. B. Lindamond, "The Underwriter Wire," *Underwriter's Report, Inc.* (December 12–18, 1997).

2. Ibid.

3. J. Robinson, *10 Facts Every Employer and Employee Should Know about Workplace Violence* (Vacacille, Calif.: The Institute of Workplace Violence Prevention, 1999).

4. *The Cost of Workplace Violence to American Business* (Palm Springs, Calif.: Workplace Violence Research Institute, 1998).

5. U.S. Department of Labor, Bureau of Labor Statistics, Office of Safety, Health, and Working Conditions, *Job-Related Homicides Profiled* (Washington, D.C., 1996).

6. "Colleague Angst Can Seethe in Next Cubical," *USA Today*, 6 September 1999.

7. *Job-Related Homicides Profiled*.

8. Ibid.

9. Robinson, *10 Facts Every Employer and Employee Should Know about Workplace Violence*.

10. C. M. Pearson, L. M. Andersson, and C. L. Porath, "Assessing and Attacking Workplace Incivility," *Organization Dynamics* (unpublished).

11. U.S. Department of Labor, Occupational Safety and Health Administration (OSHA), *Compliance Assistance Authorization Act of 1998*.

12. S. Kaufer, *Corporate Liability: Sharing the Blame for Workplace Violence* (Palm Springs, Calif.: Workplace Violence Research Institute, 1998).

13. U.S. Office of Personnel Management, *Dealing with Workplace Violence: A Guide for Agency Planners* (Washington, D.C., 1998).

14. S. Kaufer and J. Mattmen, *Workplace Violence: An Employer's Guide* (Palm Springs, Calif.: Workplace Violence Research Institute, 1998).

15. Ibid.

Chemical Guide

1. *Drug-Free Workplace Act of 1998* (Old Saybrook, Conn.: Business and Legal Reports, Inc., 1999).

Index

JAMES FEARING, PH.D., is a psychotherapist, licensed drug and alcohol abuse counselor, and crisis interventionist with more than twenty years of clinical and business coaching experience. Known as "America's Crisis Doctor," he writes and lectures extensively on the topics of addiction, depression, and personal performance. His first book, *Workplace Intervention*, was published by Hazelden in 2000. He has a doctoral degree in human behavior and a master's degree in counseling psychology and has received specialized training from Hazelden, Minneapolis Clinic of Neurology, and Antioch University. Active in professional associations and numerous nonprofit causes, he is president of National Counseling Intervention Services, Inc., which helps businesses and individuals around the world overcome and avert crises.

National Counseling Intervention Services, Inc.
11391 Ridgedale Drive, Suite 175
Minneapolis, MN 55305
(800) 279-3321
www.nationalcounseling.com
drfearing@nationalcounseling.com

HAZELDEN INFORMATION AND EDUCATIONAL SERVICES is a division of the Hazelden Foundation, a not-for-profit organization. Since 1949, Hazelden has been a leader in promoting the dignity and treatment of people afflicted with the disease of chemical dependency.

The mission of the foundation is to improve the quality of life for individuals, families, and communities by providing a national continuum of information, education, and recovery services that are widely accessible; to advance the field through research and training; and to improve our quality and effectiveness through continuous improvement and innovation.

Stemming from that, the mission of this division is to provide quality information and support to people wherever they may be in their personal journey—from education and early intervention, through treatment and recovery, to personal and spiritual growth.

Although our treatment programs do not necessarily use everything Hazelden publishes, our bibliotherapeutic materials support our mission and the Twelve Step philosophy upon which it is based. We encourage your comments and feedback.

The headquarters of the Hazelden Foundation are in Center City, Minnesota. Additional treatment facilities are located in Chicago, Illinois; New York, New York; Plymouth, Minnesota; St. Paul, Minnesota; and West Palm Beach, Florida. At these sites, we provide a continuum of care for men and women of all ages. Our Plymouth facility is designed specifically for youth and families.

For more information on Hazelden, please call 1-800-257-7800. Or you may access our World Wide Web site on the Internet at www.hazelden.org.